THE
Archive Photographs
SERIES

PRESTON

John Garlington

Town Hall, Fishergate frontage, about 1925. This staged view, portrays study in solidity. The Town Hall, blackened by almost sixty years of industrial pollution, gives an uncompromising splendour to Fishergate. The policeman of the now disbanded Preston Constabulary stands on point duty early on a Whitsun morning. His first aid badge, life saving badge and Great War wound stripe show clearly.

THE
Archive Photographs
SERIES

PRESTON

Compiled by
John Garlington

CHALFORD

First published 1995
Copyright © John Garlington, 1995

The Chalford Publishing Company
St Mary's Mill, Chalford,
Stroud, Gloucestershire, GL6 8NX

ISBN 0 7524 0334 6

Typesetting and origination by
The Chalford Publishing Company
Printed in Great Britain by
Redwood Books, Trowbridge

To Nina, Ruth and Beth.

Fishergate about 1950. With one or two exceptions, Fishergate still retains its Edwardian appearance, even down to the road surface of sets. On the extreme right are the unexpanded *Lancashire Evening Post* premises. Further down looms the spirelet of the churchlike Gas Board Offices. In the distance are the cupola of the Shelley building and the clock tower of the Fishergate Baptist Church.

4

Contents

Friargate looking South, from Heatley Street corner, probably 1946. This unusual view illustrates admirably how the Scott's Town Hall dominated Preston from 1867 to 1947 and how its clock was clearly visible by day and night when it was illuminated. Victorian shopkeepers used to send their shopboys into the street to check the time. Further down on the right the gable ended frontage belongs to the Old Black Bull which now stands on the corner by the modern ring road which cuts right across Friargate.

Opposite, above: The Christ Church section of the 1922 Preston Guild Anglican procession return to their church as the Sunday School's second girls' banner has just passed the railway station approach. The original church was eventually closed in 1970 and the remaining part of it is now used as a chapel/conference room known as Christ the King.

Introduction

This book celebrates Preston's past in photographs by showing the streets and buildings which have been well known, frequented and used as landmarks by the town's ordinary citizens, and those citizens going about their business, living their lives. This is not a book of dignitaries' portraits or a list of famous names except where they fit into the general scheme of the book. Neither is it a catalogue of glittering events such as Royal visits, though various Guilds are represented at street level. This is a collection, with commentaries, which hopes to show the modern observer an overview of Preston from about 1850 to 1950, with a special interest in the late Victorian and Edwardian periods. The topographical area covered runs from the Lane Ends at Ashton in the West to the Cemetery in the East; from the Ribble in the South to Fulwood in the North.

Every attempt has been made to make this overview as comprehensive as possible, and few topics or aspects have not been touched upon, while others illustrated here have been the subject of their own extensive histories, for example schools, and are present here as smaller parts of the greater whole.

It is also intended that this book should appeal to a wide range of people, from children, who often find old photographs fascinating, to older people who may be perhaps looking to remember places and situations which have now disappeared, and there are many of these.

The photographs come from a number of sources and took patience and heart searching to select, as the original choice would have filled almost two books of this size. Some views come from prints in my possession whose originals are held by the Harris Museum, others were lent to me from smaller private sources which are acknowledged at the end of the book. The rest of the images come from my local history collection, some of which are postcards.

It is interesting to note, however, that some photographs included here had already been consigned to the dustbin by their previous owners. Two groups were about to be thrown away before being rescued and the third, the Larkhill group, were literally pulled from a bin by a former pupil of mine.

In the early photographic section, Robert Pateson's work is the most notable and it is worth considering the conditions he worked under. Much of his equipment had to be made specially, sometimes by himself, and he had to prepare his own negatives. Commenting in 1903, when he was in his seventies, he thought that Edwardian photographers had an easy life as he had had to grind his own lenses. During the period 1857-69 the early photographers became involved in a race to move from studios at humbler addresses to town centre premises. By 1869 Pateson and Isaac Bradley were working from 51a and 41a Fishergate, respectively, shortly to be followed by John Monk and Charles Sanderson, both in Church Street, with Alfred Beattie working in Chapel Street.

I have chosen to look at the 1922 Guild Pageant because it was a work of art produced by ordinary people celebrating their past in historical drama and celebrating their, and the town's future, through their children. During the 1842 Guild, children of all denominations sang hymns and songs on the Market Place - the first children's event at any Guild. A spectacular gathering of thousands of children in Avenham Park in 1862 to sing songs and hymns was a great success. Because of religious quarrelling, only Anglican and Nonconformist children participated in a similar activity in 1882. To make something new in which all children could take part, side by side, the 1922 Pageant was devised. It is unique, as just a few years before or after this, times were financially hard and its staging would have been impossible. Its success, however, was echoed in later Pageants in 1952, 1972 and 1992. Children's involvement has now become a permanent feature.

I have included a photograph taken in 1982 by my brother Phil Garlington, the photographer, as it records everyday town shops which were demolished to make way for the Fishergate Centre. It made me think what important landmarks and buildings the town has lost in recent years. St. James's, the Public Hall and St. Mary's have been demolished, While St. Mark's and St. Augustine's are empty, unused shells. We owe it to coming generations to preserve the best. Crystal House stands as a reminder of the victory of expediency over quality and good taste and Scott's masterpiece, the Town Hall was lost forever. We are caretakers of the present - the future is over the next ridge, out of sight.

Although this is, by definition, a book of illustrations, I have tried to write informative commentaries which are intended to amuse and provoke thought as well as give interesting facts. I have brought in as much human interest as possible. As one commentator once said, "After all, a town is not just its streets and buildings, but a place where people live, work, are educated, worship and seek amusement."

Ivy Bridge about 1905. A passenger train thunders along the East Lancashire line over Ivy Bridge at the end of Derby Walk. The bridge has now been cleared of all vegetation. Under it can be seen the wrought iron gates which formed one of four gateways to the park which used to be locked at night.

One

Early Days

The Obelisk and Fish Stones, Flag Market about 1853. The obelisk, really a clustered column, was the second to stand here and the last of many similar fitments, such as market crosses, on this square before being removed and made into gateposts at Hollowforth Hall in 1853. Built in 1782 after the collapse of the original,, the obelisk was installed with a gas lamp in 1816, thus illuminating Preston's market in a unique way for the time. The fish stones, placed nearby in 1605, were also cleared away in 1853. The square was flagged in 1867.

North East corner of Winckley Square about 1855. Until 1801, most of this area was a large open space known as Town End Field which was bought by Thomas Winckley. He developed it into a square, kept apart from the rest of the town centre, which became a prestigious place to live in or near. The houses had mostly Georgian styled frontages with neo-classical doorways and patterned railings. To the left are the gardens which were held privately by the house owners who each had a key to their plot. The original photograph is a small ambrotype.

Avenham Brow, by Charles Wilson, about 1852. Between 1862 and 1864 this area became the northern part of Avenham Park designed by Mellor of London and constructed by an army of cotton workers temporarily unemployed because of the Cotton Famine. In the distance, on the left, is the Avenham side of "Ivy" Bridge and a cottage in an agricultural setting. At the bottom of the gardens ran the tramway lines beyond the stationary steam engine. The houses are on East Cliff (left) and Ribblesdale Place (right).

Avenham Valley and the Ribble photographed by Charles Wilson, about 1852. A country lane with a rustic fence leads down to the tramway. Across, through the trees, is Jackson's Cottage and Garden, which comprised of two small cultivated fields, bought by the Corporation in 1862 for their Park scheme. The Ribble is in the distance, crossed by the East Lancashire Railway bridge and the North Union further on. The latter was designed like Old London Bridge, but later rebuilding has masked its appearance.

Avenham Valley from the Vicarage garden, East Cliff c.1861 by Robert Pateson. This view complements those taken by Charles Wilson and shows Jackson's Cottage and Garden to the left. Above, on Avenham Incline, stands the chimney of the stationary steam engine. The steep, gradient from Tram Bridge to the top of the Incline shows clearly how industrial power was needed to haul up coal trucks. As a contrast, on the far, left stands Avenham Tower. The Ribble is in the swell of a high tide and across it strides Tram Bridge which has long survived its commercial use. Luxuriant trees and later landscaping prevents a similar view today.

Avenham Lane, 1862 photographed by Robert Pateson. One of the town's oldest thorough-fares, Avenham Lane was, and still is, a road of contrasts. In front of the camera, which is looking West, is a charming and prosperous scene. The bow fronted house was owned by George Sharples, a successful pharmacist of the time. In the distance are the gates of Avenham Walk and to the right is the portico of Avenham House, demolished in 1890 for road widening. Behind the camera was an area inhabited by the families of cotton workers, artisans, and labourers which worsened, the further East a person travelled.

South West corner of Winckley Square 1862 by Robert Pateson. These fine residences on the West side of the Square are all basically in the Georgian style which has made it famous among students of architecture. Number 23, with the projecting portico, was the home of Thomas Batty Addison, thought by some to be Charles Dickens' model for Josiah Bounderby in *Hard Times*. In the foreground are the gates which were closed at night and a small gate leading to a private garden. The railings were removed in 1940, but fortunately replaced fifty years later. Notice the boy on the steps of number 22.

Corner of Cross Street and Winckley Square, 1862 by Robert Pateson. This magnificent view shows Thomas Ainsworth's villa, built in an Italian style in 1850, thus completing the Square and complementing the good architectural style already there. Ainsworth was a wealthy cotton magnate with a factory off Church Street where working conditions were very harsh. In the 1940s the villa became a County Court office and was eventually demolished in 1969. Its successor is a dreadful, redbrick office block.

Winckley Square from the South East, 1862, by Robert Pateson. Looking down this side of the Square can be seen the tower of Ainsworth's villa, the minarets of the Winckley Club, and on the left, gates to the private South side. Some houses, almost all now used as offices, have been fairly carefully preserved, as has the one on the left, but some have been rebuilt without much thought, especially on this side. Serious proposals to make the Square a car park in 1970 were quashed, but traffic makes it a busy place during the day. Described in 1880 as having "emerald charm and propriety of culture" the Square still seems like a retreat from the town centre rush.

Guild Arch, Fishergate in 1862 by Robert Pateson. Ghostly figures on both sides give an idea of the long exposure needed to take this photograph. Every twenty years Preston celebrates the Guild Merchant and temporary , decorated, arches welcome visitors. To the left is the newly built Fishergate Baptist Church and opposite is the Theatre Royal. Just further on, the one storey shop, is one of the oldest in the town. The bill posters advertise the Guild Ball and an opera at the Theatre Royal. All this right side is now occupied by the Fishergate Centre.

London Road Guild Arch, looking North by Robert Pateson, 1862. Children have gathered to be photographed but have been partly thwarted by an adult. Although the town had become very industrial by this time, the horse drawn carts show that country life was not far away. Despite the Cotton Famine and wet weather the Guild was a success, especially the Trades Procession, the Children's Pageant (with 25,000 children), and the twice postponed firework display in front of 20,000 spectators. The poster on the right announces that Charles Blondin, (1824-97) was to walk a tightrope across the Marsh and Ribble, having performed a similar feat across Niagara Falls in 1859.

14

The old Town Hall in 1862 by Robert Pateson. This site, now occupied by Crystal House, is seen in the process of being cleared. In the first phase, ancient houses occupied during Guild Week celebrations were demolished. The second phase held a similar fate for the rest, including the old Town Hall (left), completed in 1782, but too small by 1862, for Council business. One clock face survived, the clock being sold to a farmer near Kirkham, and the cupola, built to house it in 1814, was relocated on the Public Hall. The new Town Hall's foundation stone was laid during the 1862 Guild celebrations.

The new Town Hall, probably 1867, by Robert Pateson. In 1860, Sir George Gilbert Scott (1811-78), the famous architect, was commisioned to design the new Town Hall to cover the whole of the area in the previous photograph. It took nearly five years to build and was formally opened on 2 October 1867, when schools were on holiday and there was great pomp and ceremony. The Town Hall was the first protagonist in the "Battle of the Styles" and dwarfed all around it with size and magnificence. Pateson has caught it while the Longridge stone was totally clean; twenty years of mill pollution darkened it considerably.

Market Square from Cheapside by Alfred Beattie 1882. Later in same year this whole site was cleared to make way for the Harris Museum and Art Gallery. There are three pubs visible: on the left is the Cross Keys, nearby is the New Bee Hive and to the right is the sign of the Blue Anchor, three short cuts out of Victorian Preston. Under number fifteen is the archway of Gin Bow Entry, leading to Molyneux Square. The Museum indirectly helped some shopkeepers to prosperity; Anthony Gardner moved his shoe business to 2 Plungington Road and 25 New Hall Lane; Joseph Hallmark relocated his ironmongers to 114 Fishergate and Clifton Street, Lytham.

Cheapside looking North, 16 July 1885 by Alfred Beattie. A mounted escort and a large crowd await the emergence from the blackened Town Hall, of the Prince of Wales, later Edward VII, during his two day visit to lay the new Dock's foundation stone. At the far end are the Commerce Buildings and other shops which were to be demolished in 1893 to make way for Market Street, the new General Post Office and improvements which opened up this area considerably. On the left is the bow front of the Castle Inn, built in 1623. Long after the Castle had gone buildings on its site retained that shape.

Shops in Fishergate near the Railway Station, probably 1897. These premises were built about 1845. Number 53, left, is the Alexandra Hotel which had recently been taken over by Hannah Richardson, the next door neighbour, in 1894. William Tuson, a draper who also sold floor coverings, owned number 54, from where trading was done under his name until 1943. Should anyone be in doubt, the Railway Drug Store was owned by John Jackson whose window is cluttered with stock. Judging by the Royal crests, Queen Victoria's Diamond Jubilee was being celebrated.

Shops in Fishergate near the Railway Station, 1982. Here are the same buildings eighty five years later. On the left is Forsyth's Jeweller's who took these premises just after the War. The centre two restaurants occupy the premises of William Tuson "linoleum and carpet dealer", offering more exotic food than in the Alexandra Hotel. A medical parallel is created with an optician occupying the old chemist's. Both these views were taken in the early morning to avoid heavy traffic. This modern picture has some historical significance because the buildings were demolished shortly afterwards to build the Fishergate centre.

Ellen Garlington at 12 St. Austin's Road, Preston, in the winter of 1861/2. Born Ellen Green in 1833, she was the daughter of Margaret and James Green, tin plate worker of Bowker Street. She married John Garlington in October 1861 at St. Augustine's R.C. Church. She had six children, her last at 46 and died in 1884 of exhaustion, as did many other Victorian women. She is wearing a gingham crinoline supported dress, rag-sleeved with undersleeves, which may have been her wedding dress. She wears a black velvet choker fastened with a jewelled pin and a fashionably severe hairstyle, centre-parted and drawn across the ears.

John Garlington at 12 St. Austin's Road, in the winter of 1861/2. Born in 1833 he was the son of Margaret and Richard Garlington, a calico printer. A cabinet maker by trade, he moved with the family to a newly developed area in Brackenbury Street in 1873. He collapsed and died in Moor Lane on his way to work in 1891. An unknown travelling photographer had called at St. Austin's Road and taken Ellen's picture. On arrival from work, John was annoyed that money they could ill afford had been spent, but still sat for his picture, in his working clothes. He is wearing a single breasted jacket over a lapelled waistcoat and fustian or moleskin trousers. Under his fringe beard he wears a low collar, fastened with a large bow tie. The resulting ambrotypes were the only photographs ever taken of this couple.

Higginson and Holderness of St. Austin's Road produced this carte-de-visite of M. Bickerstaffe (top left), probably in her confirmation dress, in the late 1860s. Isaac Bradley, who began working at the same time as Pateson in the 1850s, produced about 1869 this photograph of an unnamed woman in a very full crinolined dress (top right), and of Josephine and Frederick Hammond (bottom left), who are kept in place by clamps visible near their feet and under the girl's armpits. Charles Sanderson caught the Cussacks (bottom right) in their best outdoor clothes in 1870 at a time before he moved to his Church Street studio about 1875.

The small girl (above left), photographed by Sanderson, wears a brocaded bodice and an "Alice" band popularised by Tenniel's drawings in Carroll's "Alice in Wonderland". Beatrice Hammond, about 1893 (bottom right), wore one similar when Alfred Beattie photographed her at 10 Chapel Street, where he worked from 1873-96. Also by him (top right) is an unnamed young woman leaning on a fashionable pedestal about 1875 and (bottom left) in this unusual outside carte-de-visite, Rose Sharples wears a type of jacket made popular by Alexandra, Princess of Wales after 1863.

Two
Round The Town

Preston from Penwortham. Really intended as a photograph to record the New Penwortham Bridge constructed in 1912, the view of distant, Edwardian Preston it contains is quite valuable. On the left is the spectral, white stone finish of Christ Church; to its right are the County Offices. The two spires on the right are those of Fishergate Baptist Church and the Town Hall. The square mass on the far right is the Harris Museum.

Broadgate about 1907. Tram number 12 is about to set off for the Withy Trees at Fulwood on one of the earliest routes. Behind is the Ribble, crossed by the old bridge, constructed in 1756. Two previous ones had collapsed. The bridge is still standing, though traffic was removed from it in 1912 when the new bridge was built.

Broadgate in flood about 1912. This area, Walton-le-Dale and Frenchwood used to be prone to flooding when the Ribble burst its banks. People were drowned when their houses were overwhelmed at the turn of the century. At this time, Rule 24 of the Preston tram driver's hand book stated that trams had to stop near the new bridge if Broadgate was in flood and to turn back until officially told it was safe.

Fishergate Hill Station about 1950. Built by the ill-fated West Lancashire Railway in 1882, but surplus to the requirements of its later buyers, the Lancashire and Yorkshire Railway. It was closed to passengers in 1900, though remained a goods station until the Beeching cuts of 1964. Silcocks the feed merchants leased the offices for some years before its eventual demolition in the 1980s.

Fishergate Hill about 1912. Two trams pass each other on the Hill . The open tram waits on a loop while the other moves on a single track down to Broadgate. At the upper end of the Hill are the County Offices and opposite was Miss Ketton's Cambridge House School for girls which later became the Cambridge Hotel in 1965. The house on the left has, in recent times, been the Moose Hotel. On the right is the garden wall of number 10 West Cliff.

West Cliff about 1906. On the left, in the distance, is number 10 West Cliff, the home of Doctor Farnworth, which became Round Cliff Preparatory School for boys, run by Mr D. Farnworth MA. Like other roads, such as Spring Bank, which branched off Fishergate Hill, West Cliff was the home to many wealthy, professional and independent families including the Toulmins.

County Hall, Fishergate about 1910. The first part of County Hall was built in 1878 as headquarters of the Lancashire Constabulary and the second, including the County Hall and committee rooms, was opened in 1882. Both phases, including fittings, cost £58,000. For fifty years county magistrates met here in session and later the Council itself. After the 1902 Education Act, further extensions were needed to accommodate offices running fifty secondary schools and seven hundred elementary schools. Further building took place in 1934 along Pitt Street and Marchand Street.

Fishergate, Victoria Buildings about 1906. Frith and Sons of Reigate produced this fine view of the west end of Fishergate, showing the activity of an Edwardian Summer's afternoon. Only recently built, Victoria buildings were occupied by Richard Bomont's, hairdresser's, William Bradshaw's, opticians (see large spectacles) and Musson's, oyster dealers. Further on is Jane Wade's Bazaar. On the right are Queen's Buildings which were demolished eighty years later to accommodate the Fishergate Centre.

Victoria Buildings about 1932. Also a Frith product, this view shows the growing influence of the car as Wade's Bazaar has given way to Loxham's Garage, surmounted by the legend "The Age Of The Motorcar". Further on, is the imposing Fishergate Baptist Church, designed by James Hibbert and built in 1857-8 at a cost of £6,500. On the right is the classical facade of one of Preston's oldest shops and, further on, stands the Theatre Royal. It is interesting to compare this and the previous picture with Robert Pateson's on page 14.

Fishergate, by the Theatre Hotel c.1912. On the right is the Theatre Hotel, run by Mrs Ann McConnell, who lived on the premises. Always a very popular public house, it flourished until Boddingtons sold it in 1987 for demolition in favour of shops. The two premises further right were Reed's, auctioneers and Parker's, chemist's. E.J. Reed obviously a wealthy man, lived in Newton Road, Ashton, while Thomas Parker lived in much humbler, Frenchwood Street.

Fishergate near Fox Street c.1906. The delicate tinting of this Frith postcard ensured that no fine detail was lost. On the left, up to the ivy covered building on Fox Street corner, are the shops owned by Brocklehurst and Sons, tailors; John Frame, tourist director and James Jamieson, the photographer, who worked at these premises from 1904-1932. Richard Brocklehurst was successful and lived in Newton Road Ashton. Frames Tours left their premises in 1988, and Brucciani's cafe, sold by the family in 1991, occupied Jamieson's former premises.

Aerial view of the town centre from the West, 1922. The development of Preston from a medieval streetplan is more obvious from the air. Fishergate, on a plateau, runs parallel to the valley of the culverted River Syke, and eventually to the Ribble. To the left are the stylish Sessions House, Museum and Town Hall around the Flag Market. Further on is the Parish Church and some way behind is the distinctive shape of Grimshaw Street Church. The age of cotton is about to end but factories with their chimneys and lodges, together with many terraced houses cluster near the town centre.

Aerial view of town centre from the South East, 1922. From this angle can be seen the rest of the "Battle of the Styles" and a market in progress under canvas stalls. Fishergate bisects the scene while Friargate and Market Street diverge in the top corner. The Town Hall dominates both pictures, but opinions that it would not be seen to best advantage can be understood from this view. The white-edged roof is E.H. Booth's cafe and grocer's, now Waterstone's, and the light building at the top is the normally hidden St. George's church. Unseen at street level is the mass of small buildings and alleys hidden behind shop fronts.

Town Hall, Fishergate c.1907. Forty years of pollution have darkened the Longridge stone from its original state in Pateson's photograph. The clock used Westminster chimes which, at times, could be heard from great distances away and some people used to forecast the weather from the sound. Based on the medieval Cloth Hall at Ypres, officials from there came to see the Town Hall before rebuilding the war-shattered Cloth Hall in 1919. Partly destroyed by fire on 15 March 1947, the Town Hall remnant was cleared in 1962. Its whitewood dance floor was sold for firewood and the stone was ground down and used as reinforcement in the sea banking at Clifton.

Flag Market looking towards Friargate, September 1902. The Guild celebrations are in full swing and the town is a hive of activity. The corner on the right was rebuilt nine years earlier to widen Friargate and create Market Street. The new George Hotel, festooned with decorations, stands near the site of its old namesake, one of Preston's best eating houses. Among other ancient sites which disappeared were Anchor Weind, Fishwick's Yard, Back Lane and New Street. Market Street, custom-built for market trade, is straight and wide, leading away to the right.

Friargate near Orchard Street c.1925. This is another of Preston's ancient thoroughfares, taking its name from the small pre-Reformation priory sited nearby. On the right is Tyler's bootmakers and next door is Slinger and Sons who seemed to make and sell every sort of tool imaginable for home and work. Just beyond is the steel and glass portico of the Royal Hippodrome Theatre. Built in 1896, this theatre presented Variety, Music Hall and drama. In 1947 the Salberg Players began their repertory, putting on 365 plays, until March 1955. All these buildings were pulled down to make way for C&A in 1959.

Lower Friargate c.1906. Largely ignored by photographers in general, this gives a rare view of lower Friargate off this road ran many small alleys and streets formed in the early nineteenth century, the base for the Catholic community round St. Mary's (demolished 1993). Hill Street, Hope Street, Edward Street and Heatley Street are survivors of this period. In the distance is Adelphi Street and the Adelphi Hotel (established in 1774) stands on Fylde Street. Behind this stands Henry Shutt's Corn Mill (pulled down in 1994), one of the last reminders of the period up to 1830 when agriculture and windmills began and Friargate finished.

The Public Hall c.1910. Opened as a Corn Exchange in 1824, the main part was demolished in 1990 to make way for widening to the Ring road, opened in 1966. Originally a number of large rooms round an open court covered by a glass roof, the Exchange was radically transformed into a hall with galleries for the purpose of meetings and entertainments. After the Fish Stones were removed in 1853, a market for farm produce was held outside the Hall until the early 1960s. The glass canopies were removed about 1950.

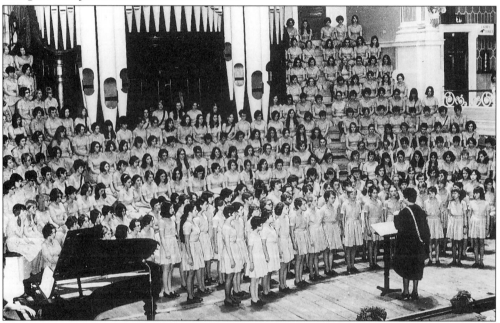

The Public Hall: Winckley Square Convent Prize Night, 3 December 1968. The Public Hall was used from 1882 to 1972, for functions such as: Guild events, balls, parish reunions, visits by the Halle and the Liverpool Philharmonic Orchestras sports, political meetings and school prize nights. It could hold 3,300 people with 300 on the stage. The organ was donated by John Dewhurst, a local coal merchant in 1881, though not played in later years. Pederewski, Pavlova, Liszt and Sousa all performed here.

The Flag Market looking North, 1903. This view of the Flag Market is very unusual. The modern view from this spot is obscured by the replaced Obelisk in 1977 and the trees which were planted in 1925. Now the area is cluttered with traffic signs and yellow lines. A year later the stanchions for tram powerlines were erected and the Boer War memorial built in front of the Post Office. The small building on the left is one of Preston's oldest buildings, built about 1640. The shadow in the foreground is cast by one of the Town Hall's pinnacles.

Whitsun Fair, Whit Monday probably 1930. The Flag Market has been put to a number of uses, Guild proclamations, public receptions, the Pot Fair and Whitsun Fairs. Taken from the great balcony of the Harris Museum, this view shows the old shops on the left and Market Street with stalls displaced from the Flag market. A modern single deck tram rubs shoulders with two buses in Friargate. The age of the bus was beginning and that of the tram was ending.

The unveiling of the Boer War Memorial, 6 October 1904. On a very wet day, crowds stood in pouring rain to witness the unveiling of this memorial which was designed in red granite and stone by the Preston sculptor, Thomas Hodgkinson. The "Loyal" North Lancashire regiment, under the command of General Baden-Powell held Kimberley against Boer attacks for four months in 1899-1900. Other Lancashire regiments fought at Spion Kop, Ladysmith and Mafeking.

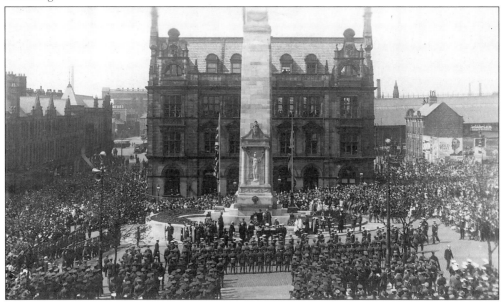

The Unveiling of the Cenotaph by Earl Jellicoe, 13 June, 1926 . Preston men served in many regiments during the Great War, but mostly in the Loyals and the East Lancs. who were present in most areas of conflict. Private William Young of the East Lancs won the V.C. in 1915. Eighteen Lancashire battalions were at the Somme on 1 July 1916, and nineteen were at Passchendaele in 1917. Both regiments bore the brunt of the last German push in 1918. Over 2,000 Prestonians died and most of their names are recorded in the Harris Museum's entrance hall. The Cenotaph was designed by Sir Giles Gilbert Scott (1880-1960).

The collapsed market roof, 6 August 1870. An area once known as "The Orchard" was developed into a large open market between Earl Street and Liverpool Street. Joseph Clayton's building firm began roofing this area in February 1870, but by 31 July only two thirds were finished. The whole structure creaked disconcertingly when it was windy, as it did during the Saturday market of 5 August. During the night the whole roof collapsed into a heap of twisted metal, if it had happened only hours earlier, there would have been hundreds of casualties. To the left is the Orchard Methodist Chapel and on the right is the Black-a-Moor Head public house.

The Covered Markets c.1925. Joseph Clayton pulled out of the contract ands a local boat builder, Thomas Allsup completed the work. His name is inscribed on the base of each pier. The original covered market is to the left across Earl Street. To the right is the Fish Market which was roofed over in 1924, at a cost of £6,000. In the early 1980s, all food stalls were moved to the new indoor market which stands on the site of the Orchard Church. The Black-a-Moor Head can be seen in the distance.

The Harris Museum and Art Gallery c.1905. On the right of the Museum is the Sessions House, completed in 1903 in the Neo-Baroque style, not yet darkened by pollution. The Museum must be the most visited non-religious building in the town. Many ancient places were destroyed to make way for it; on the other hand if this area had not been opened up and widened, modern life would have passed Preston by. Alderman James Hibbert was commissioned to design it by the Corporation and it is his crowning glory, as he intended it to be.

The Harris Museum Entrance Hall, 1902. At the Corporation's expense, Hibbert toured the Continent to see buildings designed in Ancient Greek styles, especially the work of Schinkel in Germany. Hibbert intended that the classical theme should be extended to the exhibits also, believing that an Art Museum should promote the "elevation and purification of the public taste". The foundation stone was laid in 1882 and the completed building was opened in 1891. During the next two years the Museum was closed to the public while arguments raged about financial responsibility.

Harris Museum: statues near the Rotunda, 1902. Funds for the building came from the bequest of E.R. Harris in memory of his father, the Rev. Robert Harris. However, Hibbert overspent the £100,000 and the Corporation were outraged. Some of the public were outraged also; Hibbert intended that classical sculpture should be exhibited, some being nudes which were thought to be indecent or very amusing. He declared that impurity was not in the sculptor's work, but, "…it is in (the people) themselves. It is they who bring it.".

Harris Museum: the second floor, c.1910. In the original plan there was a reading room attached to a lending library, though the reference library was on a different floor, as it is today. Collections of all types – fine arts, industrial, scientific and historical – were to have their place. Wrangling continued as Hibbert's greatest triumph led to his downfall. The corporation blamed him for overrunning the budget and he criticised their working plans for the place. Isolated in council he left for London in 1898, declaring that the Museum had fallen into "common hands".

The site of the Harris Museum in 1882 by Edwin Beattie. Edwin Beattie, an artist, passing through Preston in 1891, saw a town centre in a state of fundamental change. Ancient buildings, some in poor repair; old inns, alleys and courts, were being swept away and new streets and buildings were being designed and constructed. Interested by this and other projects, he drew and painted Preston scenes, an occupation which lasted until his death in 1917. This drawing is based on his cousin Alfred's photograph, but shows more graphically how closed in and cramped this area was.

The Market Place in 1903 by Edwin Beattie. This interesting view was optically impossible! On the left stands the new Post Office designed by Sir George Tanner in the Queen Anne style of Norman Shaw. Also opened in 1903 was the neo-classical Session House. Between the two is the Cinder Pad which was used for fairs and overflow markets. The Municipal Offices were built there in 1933. In the centre is the imposing Harris Museum; to its left is the corner of the Miller Arcade. These are the buildings which were known as the "Battle of the Styles", now weakened by the loss of the Town Hall.

Town Hall and Cheapside c.1910 by Arthur Shaw of Blackburn. Dominating this is the North side of the Town Hall, opened on 2 October 1867. Its 198 foot tower was raised one storey from the original plan so that its clock could be seen from the station. When illuminated, the clock could be seen in parts of the Fylde and from ships in the Ribble estuary. It had five bells using Westminster chimes. The largest, weighing four and a half tons, was the most powerful in Britain after Big Ben and St. Paul's. The chimes went wrong in the 1890s forcing the council to act when it struck twenty two during a morning council meeting.

The Flag Market 1952. On 15 March 1947, after a police function, fire broke out in the ballroom and quickly spread. The magnificent tower was literally its own downfall, acting like a burning chimney, drawing in air from the street. At 3.45 am the clock chimed for the last time as fire engulfed the mechanism, at which moment, the spire crashed into Fishergate. Then a great death knell sounded as falling timbers and masonry struck the bells which fell loudly, and finally, down the tower. A truncated version continued in some use until 1962. Crystal House now occupies the site.

Lancaster Road c.1910. On the left is the Miller Arcade; on the right is Starkie's Corner, so called because of Starkie's gentleman's outfitters. Past the Arcade is the East frontage and entrance to the Harris Library, and further on is the Sessions House, completed in 1903. An open space after that is the Cinder Pad where the Municipal Offices were opened in 1933. Beyond this is the balustraded tower of the Police Station. In the foreground on the right, are two of the controversial ornamental tram cable poles.

Lancaster Road Corner from Church Street c.1908. Starkie's, the outfitters on the corner boasted that their goods were sold "at the smallest possible profit", adding quickly "for ready money only". Next door is Birchall's tobacconists and next to them are the premises of Breakell and Co., a very successful wine merchant and proprietors of "Real Stingo Whiskey". They brewed beer, bottled Guinness, provided brewing materials for pubs and had a bonded warehouse in Avenham Street. The gateway on the right leads to the stables of the old coaching inn, The Red Lion, now aptly renamed The Coach House.

The Miller Arcade 1902. The Arcade covers an area originally occupied by a dozen or more premises, including part of the Old Shambles in Lancaster Road. Designed by Edwin Bush, it was opened in 1898. Covered by a terracotta facade, the structure is basically a steel frame. After being a centre of activity, its custom and appearance suffered in the 1960s. Known as Arndale House after its acquisition in 1958, the Arcade's condition caused an outcry and demolition came close in 1970. It was rescued and refurbished, its name restored, and happily it prospers today.

Church Street near Grimshaw Street c.1910. Church Street was a thriving shopping area until 1960 when commercial emphasis shifted to Fishergate, especially after St. George's Shopping Centre was opened in 1965. In Church Street in 1910 all manner of goods could be bought such as stationery, shoes, food, both cooked and fresh, drinks, alcoholic or not; anything for babies and children, smokers' requisites, medicines, herbal or otherwise, books and newspapers, musical instruments, tripe, brushes, photographs, plants and seeds.

The Prison from Church Street c.1906. Heavy traffic thunders past this point now, making the Edwardian image very rural in comparison. Notice the street sweeper in the road. The prison, built in 1789, was visited by Elizabeth Fry and John Gurney, and was found to be one of the best. In 1911 an otherwise good report revealed that there had been some cell wrecking, recommending that the best punishment would be the birch or the cat-o'-nine-tails. Closed in 1930, it was re-opened after the War and today houses about 600 inmates.

Horse trough (detail from above). Mary Cross, who founded the School for The Deaf, donated two troughs, one in Moor Lane/ North Road, and the other here at Stanley Street in May 1893. This one is combined with lamps and surmounted with a classical figure. These days it is easy to overlook the part played by horses and the hardships they suffered. A series of letters to the *Preston Guardian* in the 1880s highlighted them. One in particular described how a horse tram driver refused to heed the complaints of one lady when she pointed out that his horse's mouth was bleeding and foaming.

Three
Out And About

Deepdale Road and Stephenson Terrace c.1908. Deepdale Road may have been the road, mentioned by Doctor Kuerden between 1681 and 1687, which passed to Lancaster "...over Preston More and Fulwood...". Deepdale Enclosure, to the left, was the site of the Preston Observatory from 1881 to 1927 before its removal to Moor Park. Stephenson Terrace on the right, was completed in 1848 and survives as a listed building today. The Lodge on the left, built a year later, is no longer there.

The Royal Infirmary from Deepdale Road c.1906. The Infirmary was opened as successor to the House of Recovery and Dispensary (1809-1815) in town. Edmund Harris was a benefactor and donated a fever ward. In 1897 the East wing was added through public subscriptions. In those pre-Health service days the Infirmary relied largely on public generosity but Dr Sir Charles Brown ploughed back much of his salary to benefit patients and staff. The "Royal" title was given in 1897 and removed in 1983 when the new Hospital was opened.

The Royal Infirmary c.1905. Dr Brown was appointed medical officer in 1870, became a consultant in 1886 and retired in 1922 when he was eighty six. The Infirmary owed him a great deal. In 1898 he personally financed an operating theatre costing over £2,500. During 1902-4 he donated recreational items for staff and patients and began the nurses' annual day out to Blackpool. Most importantly he had an X-ray unit installed in 1904.

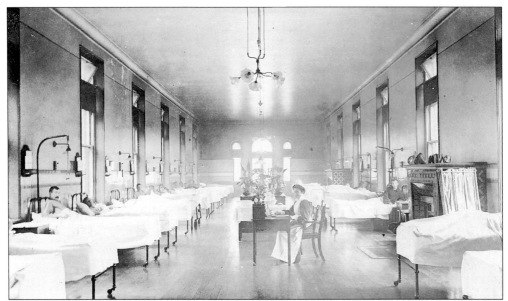

Albert Ward c.1905. A picture of perfection, as the ward sister would have wished to have it. Notice the highly polished floor, the starched linen and the bed casters all pointing the same way. The ward's simple and uncluttered appearance is unrecognisable seventy five years later. Many of these patients would directly benefit from Dr Brown's generosity. In 1905 he financed three observation wards and was knighted in 1919 for his services to health in Preston since 1865. In all, he had given over £40,000 to hospital funds.

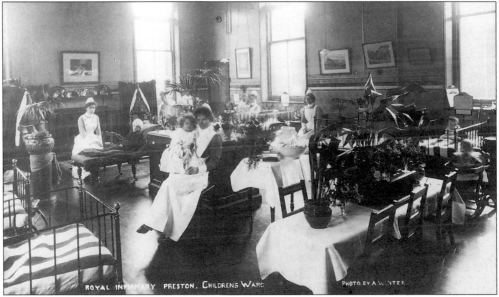

The Children's Ward c.1907. In the late nineteenth century a third of the population was under fourteen, but a children's ward was not set up in Preston until 1884. In the decade up to 1870, 14,000 Preston children died of typhoid, typhus, smallpox, cholera, scarlatina, measles and diarrhoea. The years from 1884 to 1910 saw hundreds admitted for infectious diseases, and in 1893 the ward had to be closed for a month. After the Great War, the ward was rebuilt and refitted.

Miller Park, Ivy Bridge 1902. The bridge is the dividing line between Miller and Avenham Parks where families walked on Sunday afternoons. Ivy Bridge has been stripped of its ivy for some time and it used to carry the East Lancs railway but is now totally redundant. The gates under the bridge were locked each night at dusk, as were the entrances at West Cliff and both ends of River Walk.

Miller Park: Derby Walk c.1910. Derby Walk, or Broad Walk, was part of the popular itinerary for Sunday walking for years. On the right is the Park Hotel, in the centre is the statue of Edward Stanley, fourteenth Earl of Derby, who was Prime Minister for a time. During the Cotton Famine of 1862-5 he donated £5,000 to relieve poverty in Lancashire and the statue was erected in gratitude, with £349 raised by workmen's penny subscriptions towards the £2,500 cost. When the sixteenth Earl, Guild Mayor in 1902, opposed votes for women, local suffragettes tarred the statue.

Miller Park, The Fountain, Easter Monday, probably 1906. The fountain is set on a base which is grooved to simulate wear by water. The rest is of Longridge stone depicting the seated figures of the elements - earth, air, fire and water. Surmounting the whole structure is a large shell in which the fountain jets are set. Hundreds of people, including many children, line River Walk and the paths in this photograph showing how popular the park was.

Miller Park and the Park Hotel c.1905. The Park Hotel, the magnificent lodging place for rail travellers, dominates the park. Designed by Arnold Mitchell of Oldham and built in 1881-2 at a cost of £40,000, the building was said to be too gaudy, though the Ruabon red brick and tiles have mellowed. The County Council bought it in 1958 and built an "outrageous monstrosity" of an office block next to it. The boat in the foreground is probably one of John Crook's.

Pleasure Boat Station, River Ribble 1902. To this point the river has run nearly seventy miles from its source near Ribblehead in Yorkshire. Customers on John Crook's pleasure boat landing stage turn to the camera, including the central figure who is probably the proprietor himself. An Oxford graduate, Crook, it is said, one early morning pulled a drowned body across to the Penwortham bank because a better bounty was paid there.

Avenham Park and River Ribble from Penwortham 1902. The Ribble is at full tide, and in the foreground are the lime trees planted in the mid 1860s. In the distance are the houses of professional families on Ribblesdale Place. Before 1860 the view would have been much different as cultivated fields, an orchard and Jackson's Garden and Cottage occupied the East side. Jackson also ran a bath-house with hot and cold showers. The two distant spires are the Town Hall (left) and the Parish Church.

Tram Road c.1920. Tram Road, now a pleasant walk, had a serious purpose until 1859 as the connection between the Walton Summit and Preston sections of the Lancaster Canal. Goods, especially coal, were transported in horse-drawn trucks on rails to Tram Bridge and across to Avenham. John Proctor worked during the whole thirty two year operation, doing the five mile return journey twice a day. In his time he must have travelled 200,000 miles.

Tram Bridge and Avenham Tower c.1912. Tram Bridge, or "Canal" Bridge as it was oddly but accurately named on John Myre's 1824 map, was nearly demolished in 1859 but remains today despite accidents and neglect, being rebuilt in the 1960s. On the right is Avenham Tower; on the far side, steep Avenham Incline can be seen, at the top of which the steam engine stood, lifting trucks onto flanged rails by attaching them to an endless chain over large wheels.

Tram Engine, Avenham Incline 1869. This building stood rotting in the new park for some years. Originally the engine hauled trucks up the six-in-one Incline to continue their journey across the top of Avenham Valley, over the now culverted River Syke, crossing what is now a car park, through a tunnel under Fishergate to the Canal basin near Corporation Street. Apart from the relic of a bridge pier in a Mount street garden, nothing remains of the Preston tramway system.

The Belvedere and Avenham Tower c.1904. The engine house was boarded up and left until 1869 when it was demolished. The Belvedere was moved close by after removal in 1873 from Miller Park for the Derby statue. This view shows it and the Tower seemingly in close proximity though the Tower stands much further away on Bushell Place/Avenham Walk corner. Trees and another house have been "edited" out of this odd but interesting view.

Avenham Park c.1910. This unusual shot shows the upper part of the natural amphitheatre which has made the park popular for 130 years for entertainments and recreations such as Guild celebrations and pageants, concerts of all kinds, displays, stunts and religious gatherings. Down by the River, diving and boating were popular. The Park was laid out between 1864 and 1865 by unemployed cotton operatives during and just after the Cotton Famine during the American Civil War.

Avenham Park, Easter Monday 1912. On 9 April gales and rain ruined the morning, but on a brightening afternoon an estimated 40,000 turned out on both parks. Here are several thousand people enjoying a welcome break from the factory or shop. Among the crowd are many children who have come for egg rolling or "pace egging", when painted hard-boiled eggs were rolled down the hill until broken, and eaten.

The Resited Boer War Memorial c.1930. The memorial was dismantled and resited here in Avenham Park by the main avenue where there is a parade each February to commemorate the 124 Preston men who died in South Africa, mainly during the relief of Kimberley. The Memorial overlooks the Valley with its beautiful slope, an oasis from urban activity, a quiet, preserved rural setting.

1845. AVENHAM PARK, PRESTON.

Avenham Park Preston.

M&Q Series.

View of Avenham Park from the Belvedere Roof c.1900. On the left is the imposing Park Hotel which won Arnold Mitchell £200 for his design in 1880. A year earlier, Anthony Hewitson, a local author, called Avenham Park "....a beautiful, sloping smoothly grassy and border ornamented recreation ground....much frequented by children...they may be seen rolly-pollying [sic] down its banks and running in its hollows." Nothing much has changed, except this view is no longer possible due to the growth of trees.

Avenham Walk, 1902. This outstandingly atmospheric photograph shows the Walk, first laid out in 1696 (then known as "Aenam Walk") and given its modern appearance in 1844. It was a very popular promenade in Edwardian and Victorian times, though Hewitson remarked in the 1880s, "...looking from Avenham Walk that glorious landscape smiles in all the splendour of a rich spring tide. Here are dainty folk... walking as usual... and only now and then a workless operative trails by with a chastened look".

The Harris Institute c.1905 . The Institute was opened in October 1850 as the "Institute for the Diffusion of Useful Knowledge". By 1882 it was short of money and decaying, but was rescued by £40,000 from E.R.Harris's will. James Hibbert's 1882 extensions included laboratories, which made the Institute a centre of science until 1932. Known as the Art College to many, the Institute is now part of the University. The front rooms have some very early examples of double glazing (1850) to shut out the noise from the stationary steam engine on Avenham Incline.

The Parish Church of St. John c.1905. The first church on this site was established in the sixth century and dedicated to Saint Wilfrid because of his strong connection with the town. Every year in October his statue was paraded on horseback. The Reformation brought a change of name, though locals still call it "St. Wilfrid's". Like many ancient churches, St. John's had serious problems with its structure and graveyard. In 1770 the roof and North side fell down, and in 1810 its dangerous tower was lowered.

Parish Church interior 1914. A church rate was set for a steeple but no-one seemed keen to pay it. Developments in other quarters probably provoked change. St. Ignatius's church had a spire and a striking clock, and by 1851 the great nave of St Walburge's had taken shape. In 1853 the Parish Church was demolished and this modern, well-proportioned building replaced it. In 1972 the building was cleaned inside and out, and the side galleries removed.

Wilfrid's Catholic Church, Chapel Street, 1907. St Wilfrid's was only the seventh place of worship to be built in Preston since 900. Though its appearance was simpler than illustrated here after rebuilding between 1877 and 1879. The church was established in 1793 by Fathers Morgan and "Daddy" Dunn who were both able to empathise with rich and poor alike, which made them very popular. Through their influence, the Catholic community was pulled together; Father Dunn arranged two censuses and raised money from the rich, earning him the title of "the best beggar in England" from one peer.

Interior of St. Wilfrid's, 1902. St Wilfrid's had to be registered in 1795 as prescribed by the 1791 Relief Act, a sign that religious suspicion was still very prevalent. The original interior had galleries lit by fan light windows and there were no supporting pillars. The rebuilt church has no galleries but has massive Shap granite columns to support the roof. Fathers Dunn (d. 1827) and Morgan (d. 1814) are buried under the sanctuary, both loved by many of all religious persuasions. St. Wilfrid's is a busy church today, as in Fr. Dunn's day.

St Ignatius's Catholic Church, Meadow Street, 1913. In 1810 there were 3,500 Catholics in Preston and 5,100 by 1820. In 1834, 3,500 were cramming into three Masses at St Wilfrid's and St Mary's on Sundays, projecting a possible population of about 8,000. As a result, St Ignatius's was built in 1833 in open fields, ready for growing urban expansion and activity. It was the first church between the Lune and the Ribble to have a spire and its 117 foot structure must have looked remarkable. A baptistry and Lady Chapel, flanking the tower, were added in 1912.

St Ignatius's Church Interior, 1913. The church was blessed and opened in 1836, but consecration only came in 1929. Because of the increasing population, Joseph Hansom (1803-1882) was commissioned to extend the North end, building four extra arches and opening up the transepts. The original architect, J.J.Scholes (1798-1863) was understandably upset. His design, however, lacks the spaciousness of Hansom's extensions. Originally a Jesuit church, the Society of Jesus left in 1958 in favour of secular priests, who in turn were replaced by Carmelites in 1985.

St Ignatius's, funeral on 1 August 1911. The funeral of Fr. Butterworth S.J., killed in a motor accident, brought out hundreds of parishioners to pay their respects. On the right is part of St Ignatius's Square and the entry to St Ignatius's Place. There, at number 3, Aloysius Smith alias "Trader Horn", the famous traveller and raconteur, was born in 1861 and lived here into the 1870s. Gerard Hopkins, the Jesuit poet (1844-1889), worked in the parish for part of Lent 1882. The poet Francis Thompson (1859-1907) was baptised here.

St Ignatius's, War Memorial unveiling, 26 March 1922. By 1917 the parish had decided a memorial was needed as 120 men had been killed (rising to 228 in 1918). A penny fund was started and £150 was raised for an outdoor memorial with all the names inscribed. In the presence of a huge crowd it was unveiled by Colonel John Shute C.M.G., D.S.O., and a year later a memorial window was put in the Lady Chapel. The house on the extreme right, number 12, was once occupied by Francis Thompson's parents. Note the dark colour of the once white church extensions built in 1912.

St Peter's C.E. Church, Fylde Road c.1905. St Peter's was a "Waterloo" church financed by French Napoleonic debt and built in open fields in 1825 at a cost of £12,500. Thomas Rickman designed the building incorporating cast iron columns and window tracery. The spire was added on top of the tower in 1852. Streets grew rapidly round St Peter's as Adelphi became one of Preston's most populated districts. In 1831 there were over 33,000 people in Preston and by 1852 there were 70,800. During the 1960s the Corporation demolished all of Adelphi area and the church closed in 1973.

St. Peter's, the Minton Floor. The building was acquired by the Polytechnic, now the University, to be its Arts Centre. Under the supervision of the Centre co-ordinator, Trevor Lloyd, an old carpet in the vestry was lifted. Underneath was a magnificent encaustic tile floor commemorating Ellen German, wife of a wealthy millowner. Peter Hancock, an architect, identified the tiles as being designed by Augustus Welby Pugin and first produced by the latter's friend, Herbert Minton, in Stoke. Minton was the first to fire encaustic tiles in 1842 and examples can be seen at Osborne House, York Minster and here at St Peter's.

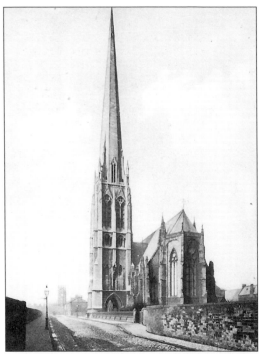

St Walburge's Catholic Church, Maudlands c.1906. "Maudlands" is a corruption of "Magdelan's Lands", referrring to the medieval leper hospital of St Mary Magdelan on whose land St Walburge's stands. Skeletons found in 1847 during foundation excavation were reburied under the high altar. Built as an offshoot of St Wilfrid's, St Walburge's served a large working class parish which numbered 1,300 families in 1906. Money was raised by door to door collection and by famous bazaars, which yielded a fantastic £8,162 between 1847 and 1852.

St Walburge's Interior c.1910. The doors were opened for Mass on 3 August 1854 and the interior the congregation saw then, is largely what is there today. The Decorated Gothic structure, designed by Joseph Hansom, measures 55 feet by 165 feet, with a view unobstructed by pillars. The roof rises 83 feet from the parapet and is supported by external buttresses working into a magnificent hammerbeam roof. In 1863 a large rose window donated by Mary Roper, was set in the West end.

Jubilee of St Walburge's 1904 by Edwin Beattie. The Golden Jubilee was enthusiastically celebrated by the parish in 1904 with a week of events. Parishioners always felt a strong sense of community and that the church was theirs because they contributed from the start. Mass was said as each venture was completed, e.g., the laying of the foundation stones in the school (1847) in the church (1850) ; the raising of the spire's cross in 1866. Hansom always felt he was only one of many working for the church.

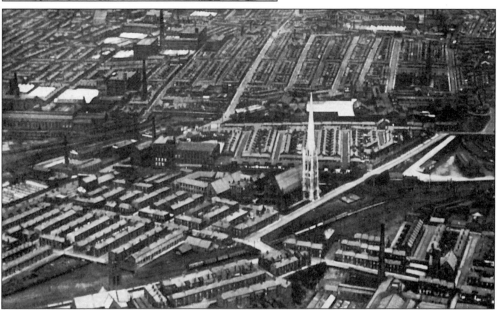

St Walburge's, an aerial view. After the Great War the parish raised money for a huge memorial for the 151 men killed, which was opened in 1923. Money left over was used for other church artifacts and a shrine to Our Lady of Lourdes. In 1853 there were doubts about building a spire, but parish pressure was insistent. It took three years to complete the 309 foot limestone structure, surmounted by a fifteen foot cross, completed in 1866. Hansom always hoped the church would become a cathedral and many consider it his masterpiece.

Garstang Road looking South c.1914. In the distance can be seen the crossroads with Addison (Blackpool) Road and the trees on the left mark the corner of Victoria Road. In the early part of the last century this road was improved between Preston and Lancaster. The section between Moor Lane and the Withy Trees was widened in 1817, getting rid of all the hillocks and depressions which made travelling so tedious and dangerous.

Garstang Road looking North, 1914. The group presents a selection of pre-War gentlemen's fashions and the police sergeant displays his stripes, first aid badge and seniority chevron. Behind him is the corner of York Avenue. This section of Garstang Road was created to avoid Black Bull Lane Hill, where horses' hooves did not grip properly in Winter. At one time it took two hours to reach Garstang, but this new link to Sharoe Green helped to reduce the time.

Withy Trees Crossroads Fulwood, c.1925. Taken from the garden of Fulwood Methodist Church, this view shows Garstang Road, from left to right crossing, with Watling Street Road running over to Lytham Road (called Watling Street Road West until 1912). In the left is Withy Trees garage demolished in the 1970s to be replaced with a more gaudy arrangement. To its left are two houses called Withy Grove, built in 1879, and in the centre is the Withy Trees Hotel, built in the early nineteenth century.

Withy Trees Hotel,

. . FULWOOD, PRESTON.

Proprietor: Fred C. Brown.

ALES, STOUTS (Draught or Bottled), WINES, SPIRITS, CIGARS, &c., all of the Best.

BILLIARDS !
BOWLING !

THE STIRRUP CUP is an institution now of ages past. But all the same, a good liquor needs no booming, and FRED BROWN, Withy Trees Hotel, sells absolutely the best of everything. Whether it be to " welcome the coming or speed the parting guest," you'll find him just the same—always pleasant and amiable. Call once, and you are sure to call again.

What can be more enjoyable, after the exhilaration of a morning or afternoon ride or drive, than the refreshment and additional exhilaration to be derived from the consumption of a glass of good Beer or Whisky. We venture to inform both riders and pedestrians, who may chance to find themselves in the vicinity of

Withy Trees Hotel, Fulwood,

Fred Brown's Guild Souvenir Advertisement, 1902. Fred Brown aimed his advertisements at "passing trade", especially cyclists and motorists. It has been said that Preston is full of pubs and churches. Between the Licensing Acts of 1872 and 1905 there were 388 licensed premises in the area and 15 of them stood on Fishergate between the Parish Church and the station. After 1905, 121 pubs were lost, including the Shepherd's Inn which stood between the Unicorn and the Moorbrook on North Road.

Watling Street Road, 1907. The houses on this wide suburban road were occupied by wealthy families such as number 6 where William Strickland Heane, successful stationer and prolific postcard publisher, lived. This postcard view, however, is not one of his but a Frith production. Tram 23 is seen running the Fulwood Inner Circle route, moving along the single track towards Withy Trees, past the loop at West Road.

The Workhouse, Watling Street Road c.1905. About this time the most populated area of Fulwood lay between this road and Eaves Brook. The Roman road from Ribchester ran along the line of Watling Street Road to Kirkham, intersecting with another road road near the Withy Trees. The Workhouse was opened on this controversial site in 1868, serving Preston, Walton and Penwortham. The misery associated with this sort of institution persisted until 1928 when it became a civic hostel. In 1979 it became the offices of the local health authority.

CTORIA ROAD, FULWOOD.   NEAR PRESTO

Victoria Road from Garstang Road c.1903. The horse-drawn buses and later trams, used this road, emerging onto Watling Street Road by East Road. Originally farmland, the whole area, known as Fulwood Park, was developed by a freehold land society enabling forty shilling freehold men to obtain the vote. Because Victoria Road was at the heart of the Park, whose boundaries were Eaves Brook, Watling Street Road, Park Walk, and Garstang Road, it was used as its main road.

Woningworth (later The Priory) 1950. One of the main instigators of the Fulwood park scheme in 1851 was the successful land agent Richard Veevers who took a number of plots for his house, "Woningworth", which was set in extensive gardens with conservatories and greenhouses. The house, which he designed, was completed in 1859 and was used by his extended family and four servants.

Woningworth, the Main Hall. Fulwood Park became a fashionable but exclusive area, a good carriage ride out of town. Veevers set up a horse-bus service in 1859, superseded by horse-trams in 1879, and he designed Christ Church on Albert Road. Being very wealthy he was able to travel abroad and have two homes. "Oakhill", his Lakeland retreat, was where he died in 1901. Rev. Abbott Peters, who was the next occupier, changed the name to "The Priory".

Plum Pudding Hill c.1906. Officially known as Park Walk, this footpath is part of an ancient thoroughfare across the Moor, extending from Watling Street Road across Moor Park to Meadow Street. In 1906 this fertile area round Eaves Brook was put to commercial horticulture. On the left are the greenhouses of Samuel Manley, gardener and florist, and on the right is Chapman Road Nursery, owned by Charles Irvin. The latter is now occupied by houses, the former is clear of greenhouses but overgrown.

BLACK BULL LANE   FULWOOD.

Black Bull Lane c.1930. Until 1820 Black Bull Lane, or Cadley Road, as it was called, was the main route to Lancaster. The main road turned left after the Withy Trees toll bar before turning right into the valley of Savick Brook in Cadley Road. In winter the road was often impassable as horse-pulling heavy vehicles, especially important stage coaches, could not grip the surface on the inclines, causing many delays. The problem was solved by constructing the Withy Trees/Sharoe Green section of Garstang Road.

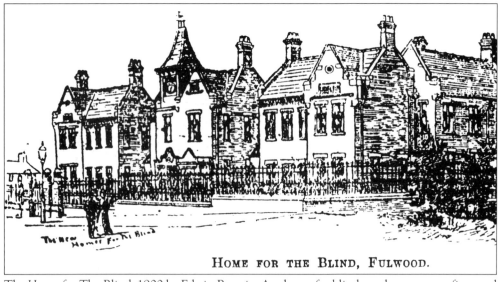

HOME FOR THE BLIND, FULWOOD.

The Home for The Blind, 1900 by Edwin Beattie. A scheme for blind employment was financed in 1864 by Joseph Livesey, the famous Preston abstainer. It was such a success that a number of premises were outgrown before the home was opened in 1895. Dormitories were built and resident scholars were taken in. Blind and partially sighted children were evacuated here from Liverpool in 1939, but only the blind returned in 1945, when the school specialised, successfully, with partially sighted pupils. Despite parental resistance, the school was sold and converted into offices.

64

Four

Day By Day

Old Yellow Mill, Preston.

Horrockses Yellow Factory built in 1792. Although handloom weaving and hand spinning had been carried out in Preston for many years, the first factory was built in 1777 and the factory system had begun. John Horrocks built the Yellow Factory and three others before 1802 and his empire was well set by his death in 1804. His brother Samuel, who lived at Lark Hill House, took over and Thomas Miller (linked with the Arcade and Park) became a partner.

Operatives leaving Horrockses Mill c.1905. Although cotton dominated the town's economy, Preston was never totally dependent on textile, and especially not after 1865, but it was a major employer. When times were bad the town became a focus of unrest and there were riots in 1808, 1818 and 1831. In 1842 when eight were wounded and five killed by soldiers in Lune Street. Strikes against wage reductions and the ensuing lock-outs caused great misery and ill feeling.

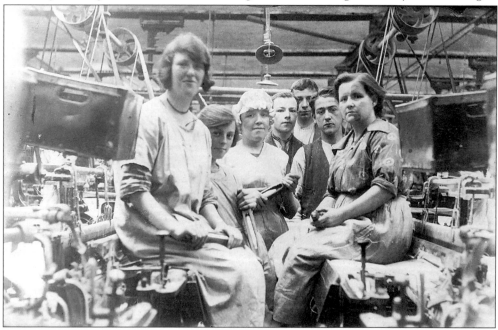

Operatives in Horrockses Mill, 1910. The American Civil War caused the Cotton Famine as the Union Navy blockaded Confederate ports, stopping raw cotton from reaching Lancashire. Thousands of people were forced to accept parish relief and many men worked for a pittance on the new Avenham Park, the Cattle Market in Brook Street and the Canal Yard. Cotton reappeared in 1865, but foreign competition in the 1870s forced Preston Corporation to invest in other industries than textiles.

An aerial view of Preston from the East c.1920. Further riots occurred in 1878 during another wage reduction strike. There were lock-outs in twenty eight factories in April, the Mayor read the Riot Act in May and the operatives were forced to return to work in June. About 37,000 Preston people worked in cotton mills at this time. From then until 1914 the industry enjoyed its last period of real prosperity, though other industries were encouraged to expand.

Cotton operatives at Horrockses Mill, 1910. After the Great War there was a rush to buy cheap cotton which had been scarce, so there was a small boom until 1921. As a result, firms took advantage of cheap labour and used outdated machinery to make short term profits. The American cotton industry re-equipped, Lancashire trained operatives worked cheap, double shifts and India put up tariffs against Lancashire cotton. Decline firmly set in when Manchester merchants began importing cheap, foreign material.

Tulketh Mill, Ashton, 1920. This interesting view shows the mill's rural situation, though streets were laid out close to it soon after 1920. The railway can be clearly seen and the Cattle Market beyond it. The white building is St Cuthbert's Church and in the top corner is the cluster of buildings at Withy Trees. The mill itself was built in 1905 in a new "Golden October" of cotton. The author's great-grandfather, Henry Myerscough, worked at Tulketh as a mill manager until about 1930.

Tulketh Mill chimney maintenance, 1925. The factory was the spinning half of a twin scheme with weaving which was never built, though extensions were made in 1918. At its peak in 1930 the mill worked 126,864 mule spindles and 12,000 ring spindles to spin American and Egyptian (sakel) yarn. Its lodges both held 1,750,000 gallons of water and the machinery was powered by a 2,000 hp horizontal cross component engine. The building is now used by the Peter Craig mail order firm.

George Moss's Bicycle Shop, 1921. Under the shadow of Horrockses Centenary Mill, on the corner of Arch Street, stood the original enterprise where George Moss bought out Holmes, cycle dealers, at 47 New Hall Lane in 1919. Cycling was popular before 1914 and demand was sufficient to sustain thirty seven dealers in Preston. After 1925, stocking a "tremendous selection" proved a success and he bought and adopted the butcher's shop at number 49 and refitted his original premises.

George Moss's Bicycle Shop, 1935. This view shows the extent of the firm's expansion, and Miller's bicycle shop at number 51 may have disappeared because of the competition. At about this time he bought a house out of town at Hesketh Bank. Between the Wars there were forty seven dealers in the town, though only eighteen remained in 1963, and Moss's remained one of the most successful, finally closing in 1982.

Preston Co-operative Society, Brackenbury Street store, 1902. The first attempts to set up a co-operative society in Preston, in 1862, failed but a further venture was successful in 1873. The Society built corner shops in the most populated areas, selling meat and groceries at competitive prices and giving a dividend. By 1905 there were twenty two stores and a central store in Ormskirk Road. Before the Great War the branches made sales worth nearly £300,000 a year.

Central Stores and Lancaster Road c.1955. Apart from the retail side, the Society ran classes, lectures and reading rooms, contributed towards the Infirmary and special needs schools, and ran a popular annual field day. In addition to the usual wares the society had a furnishing department, an abattoir, stables and coal departments. In 1916 the author's grandmother, Ann Myerscough (nee Anderton) became the first woman to be employed by the Society (at Marsh Lane). Four branches remain in 1995 after a massive decline caused by supermarket competition.

Preston Dock c.1905. It is a known fact that the Ribble estuary silts up easily, but the Corporation pressed ahead with plans to build a dock in the 1880s. Preston had always been a small shallow water port, but by 1830 most river pilots were reluctant to risk larger draught vessels. On September 1884, Alderman James Hibbert spoke against the dock scheme as "....an adventure beyond our proper province...never likely to pay...one the Corporation should never have embarked into...".

Preston Dock about 1950. In spite of a ratepayers protest, the scheme went ahead, opening in 1892. The port made a profit in its first two years. Although it became a busy concern, importing woodpulp, China clay, timber, grain and petroleum, it never made another profit. dredging had to be started in 1909 and optimism rose. The Dock Offices were opened in 1936 and new dock gear was bought. Despite pioneering the "roll on/roll off" road traffic service, profits proved elusive. Hibbert had been right; the Dock closed in 1981.

Preston Grammar School, Cross Street, c.1905. Effectively begun in 1468, the school was run in premises near the Parish Church until 1841 when new buildings, designed in the Perpendicular style with Moorish domes by John Welch, were opened. Thomas Duckett carved the decorations including the school badge, the portcullis. The whole building and contents were bought in 1860 by the Corporation for £1,500. On the left are Sir Robert Peel's statue and the Winckley Club and Philosophical Society buildings (see photograph p.13).

Preston Grammar School, Moor Park Avenue, 1913. Over the years the 1841 premises became too small and the school moved, in 1913, to a new situation near Moor Park, which had laboratories, a gym, an art room and larger classrooms. There was also a remarkable hall with an organ donated by Dr Sir Charles Brown. A magnificent War Memorial window was installed in 1925 and the small stone gateway (see above) was rebuilt outside in 1932. Further extensions were made up to 1966 as the school expanded, but in 1967 the school was wound up in the reorganisation of Preston education and is now occupied by Moor Park High School.

The Park School For Girls, Moor Park Avenue, 1910. Although some Preston senior schools were built in piecemeal fashion, the Park School was built by Woolfall and Eccles of Liverpool in 1907 as a complete unit with fifteen classrooms; chemistry, physics and botany laboratories; rooms for art, music and cooking; a school garden, tennis courts and playgrounds, both open and covered. The youngest pupils were educated at 5 Winckley Square, the home of the school's predecessor, Preston High School. The school had had only three headmistresses before reorganisation closed it in 1967. The Art Department of Preston College is now based in the building.

Royal Cross School for Deaf Children, Brockholes Brow, 1902. The school was built with £5,000 donated by Mary Cross of Myerscough and opened by the Earl of Derby in 1894. During the Edwardian period, 90 children boarded in and the school provided education for hearing impaired children for nearly a hundred years. In 1990 the school, now known as the Royal Cross Primary School, moved to new premises in Ashton. The approach used nowadays in educating these children is "total communication", using both sign language and English for the first time.

The Harris Orphanage, Garstang Road, 1902. An area in Fulwood called Crow Trees was bought for £4,800 in 1881 and £100,000, given from the will of E.R. Harris, paid for the orphanage building opened in 1888. Instead of using a communal system, the children were put into house groups under house parents. By 1918 the orphanage ran three houses each for boys and girls and extensive educational resources were in use. A change of name came, in 1946, to Fulwood and Cadley Council School and a change of direction pointed it into primary education after 1953. Falling rolls forced the school to merge and move away in 1979. The University now uses the buildings as halls of residence.

St Vincent's Catholic Poor Law School, St. Vincent's Road, 1900, by Edwin Beattie. This large turreted, red brick establishment was opened on the East side of Garstang Road in 1896 with room for 300 boys. A sum of £6,000 was needed for the project and a Grand Bazaar at the Public Hall raised £7,179 in November 1891. Run by the Sisters of St. Vincent de Paul, St. Vincent's performed a great social and educational service for deprived boys until it was closed in 1961. A small remaining part of the school is still used by Corpus Christi R.C. High School.

74

St. Ignatius's Higher Grade School, 1905. From the mid-Victorian period to the Great War there was a massive and intense educational undertaking in St. Ignatius's parish. By 1896 over 1,300 pupils attended St. Ignatius's Infants', Boys', Girls' and Higher Grade Schools. All these regularly received the highest commendations from the Education Department, with the Higher Grade being recognised especially for its prowess in commercial studies. The building in the background was demolished in 1983.

St. Ignatius's Boys School c.1905. By 1905, Alderman Richard Myerscough, a former pupil of the schools and a former parishioner, was able to declare that six of the seven Catholic Preston councillors had been educated at St Ignatius's schools. The Xaverian Brothers ran the Boys' School for nearly fifty years before they left in mysterious circumstances, involving religious-political manoeuvring, in 1900, much to the regret of the parishioners. The schools continued to flourish until local street demolitions in 1964. The old Girls' School now houses the present Junior School.

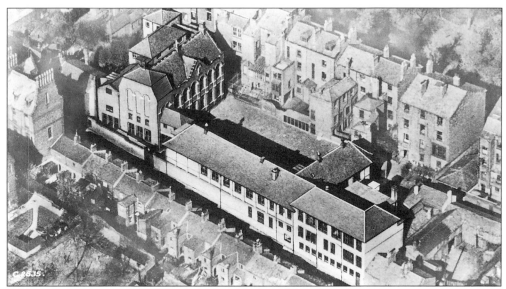

The Catholic College c.1935. This aerial view shows the buildings that the college occupied up to the last War, but before and after this time the school occupied all the houses on Winckley Square (background) between Garden Street (number 25) and the school front door (number 34), with the exceptions of nos. 30-32. One of these, number 27, had been the house of Dr Sir Charles Brown, bought after his death. The school expanded to its full extent between 1950 and 1970 when there were 900 boys educated there. The buildings to the left housed the hall and, below, were classrooms. The buildings on Mount Street (foreground) contained classrooms, swimming pool (opened 1936) and well equipped laboratories.

The Old Staff Room, 1910. Mr Harold "Plum" Wilson B.A., teacher and school secretary 1902-1912, enjoys a pipe in a room later abandoned in favour of a more central location. The college was opened in 1865 by the Society of Jesus, based at St Wilfrid's, in a house in Mount Pleasant with eleven pupils, moving in 1879 to number 29 Winckley Square. From here came the use and adaptation of buildings between Mount Street and Winckley Square. The Society adopted the policy of raising a loan, building, then mortgaging the finished product for a fixed term to release future generations from overhanging debt.

By the covered playground, Third Form Class with Rev Fr Page. The period from 1897 to 1904 was a time of expansion, and at the end the College was recognised as a Secondary School, with 126 boys. A tenth of the old boys who fought in the Great War were killed (54). By the time the War Memorial was installed in the hall (1920), the College had 300 pupils. Fifty one old boys were killed in the last War. After 1950 the school reached a peak in academic achievement, especially the period 1961-73. As part of educational reorganisation, the school was absorbed into Newman College and left its premises in 1986.

First Eleven by the Hall building, 1920. In 1961 the college took part in local sports competitions for the first time, which resulted in great success over the years. The Houghton Shield for cricket and Lucas Shield for football were won regularly. One of the Preston North End "Invincibles", Fred Dewhurst, taught English and Maths at the College. He scored in the 1888 and 1889 FA Cup Finals and brought the Cup back in 1889 for all the boys to drink lemonade from. He also scored the first League goal on 8 September 1888.

Lark Hill House School, Preston, 1903 by Edwin Beattie. After his brother John's death, Samuel Horrocks took over the textile empire and needed a house which befitted his great wealth and station. The bow fronted section of the convent school buildings constitutes the original mansion built during 1796-7, and named Lark Hill House. South facing and looking over grassland, a lake and a screen of now luxuriant trees, it was much admired and featured in architectural publications over the 1820-50 period. Life seems to have been eventful here; a mob attacked Lark Hill in 1812; Samuel Horrocks Senior received a death threat and an attempt on his life; but also there were balls and social gatherings.

Lark Hill, The Avenue, 1908. Samuel Horrocks died in 1842, aged 76, followed by his son four years later, aged 49. From then on the house was not regularly lived in and was sold in 1860 for £4,525 to St Augustine's parish, assisted by wealthy Catholic merchants. A school was needed for girls and the Faithful Companions of Jesus accepted Lark Hill as their convent and they provided teachers for the Poor Schools, a boarding and day school and a pupil teacher centre. The arrangement worked and modifications were made to the house in 1870.

Lark Hill, the house and chapel, 1908. In August 1893, work began on the block to the left to provide two new classrooms and a music area with practice cubicles. On the second floor were a chapel (damaged by fire in 1972)and a dormitory. The original portico and West entrance to the house were rebuilt facing South. In 1900 the whole building was converted to electricity and a building fund was set up in 1907. A three day mammoth fancy fair raised enough money for work to start on improvements and extensions that same year.

Lark Hill, the Seniors' Study Hall, 1908. This now forms part of Cardinal Newman College Library. The school was accepted as a Direct Grant School in 1919 after satisfying certain conditions e.g. building a science laboratory. The greatest addition was made in 1932 which is the large three-storeyed building, including the hall, which visitors see first on entering the gate. The school moved from strength to strength with rising pupil numbers after the last war. After 1967 Lark Hill took students from the Catholic high schools and did not admit junior pupils after 1977. Since 1986 Lark Hill has been the home of Cardinal Newman College into which the Sixth Form was absorbed.

Winckley Square Convent School at 23, 24, and 25 Winckley Square, 1938. In 1868 the Taunton Commission found that girls' education was severely lacking in many areas; too much time spent on accomplishments, not enough on the basics, and what was taught was badly done. In other words, women of all classes were being given a raw deal. In order to redress the situation as far as Catholic girls were concerned, the Order of the Holy Child Jesus (founded 1846) made it their aim to provide the appropriate primary and secondary education.

Winckley Square Boarders, 1909. Some of this group of Sixth Formers and Pupil Teachers are wearing the latest thing - wrist watches. When the nuns arrived in Preston, dressed as servants or widows to avoid anti-Catholic feeling, they set up small convent schools at St Walburge's (1853), St Mary's and English Martyrs (1871). In 1875 the schools at the first three were brought together at 23 Winckley Square and a century of academic and educational excellence was begun. Number 23 had been the home of Thomas Batty Addison, formerly the Recorder of Preston. (See also p.12).

Winckley Square, the Garden Street Buildings c.1950. During the next four decades the school expanded in two directions, occupying the whole block between East Cliff and Garden Street. In the Edwardian period increasing pupil numbers and the expanding nature of educational aims forced further extensions. In January 1909 the red brick building in Garden Street (above)was opened, the hall (below) was extended and the library re -equipped and enlarged.

The School Hall, Senior Oxford Examinations, 1909. In 1896 the first public examination, the Preceptor's Examination, was taken by a Sixth Formers, and a small special group prepared for Oxford Local Examinations in 1902. Finally, in 1906, pupils were entered for the Oxford at all levels. This odd photograph was taken on the great day when the school became a centre for Oxford Local Examinations. The girls' faces have strained and serious expressions, not unlike those children today taking their annual examinations!

Our Lady's Corridor, 1910. This postcard view and the following two come from a larger sequence used by the school for correspondence purposes and for advertise the facilities for day and boarding pupils. This corridor, on the first floor, ran the full length of the 1909 developments on Garden Street and was known as Our Lady's Corridor with the statue set in a large bow window at the far end. On the left are the windows overlooking the playground, on the right are the new classrooms.

The School Library, 1910. This area formed part of the first floor of number 23 and was originally the school hall. As numbers of pupils grew conditions became more cramped and two classes had to be housed in and around this area in 1894. In the decades after 1909 the library was extended behind the Edwardian photographer's position, which made it five times as large, much of it overlooking the Square.

The Science Room. The Convent H.C.J., Winckley Square, Preston.

The Science Room, 1910. One of the most contentious educational issues over the years has been over the amount of science taught to girls. The school built rooms specifically for Chemistry and Physics in 1909, being very advanced for the time. In 1887 the school had become a Science Centre when other schools only dallied with the subject. Secondary Schools Regulations, issued in 1904 insisted that more time be spent on Chemistry and Physics, and Botany was added to the curriculum. Biology was included in 1920.

The School Uniform and May Waring, January 1914. In the early days of the school there had been no uniform, but after 1909, the school wore navy dresses in Winter, in Summer, royal blue dresses (denim for a time) and white blouses with black shoes without any prescribed style. The school colours changed in 1956 to green, and grey after 1963. In 1875 there were 90 pupils at the school, rising to 140 in 1906, 165 in 1909 and 342 in 1926. In 1946, 604 scholars attended the school, rising to a peak of 850 in 1962.

Pupils in Garden Street, Summer 1962; competition entry by T. Proctor. This and the following view were found in a drawer when the school was closed in 1981. The majority of pupils came from Preston but many also came on County scholarships. Families of all financial backgrounds could send their daughters to receive an education which was enriched by many extra-curricular activities. In 1978 the school was absorbed into Newman College and closed in 1981. The old premises are now occupied by offices, a free newspaper and a restaurant. The library, which had over 11,000 books was made over to Newman College.

Pupils in the yard 1962; competition entry by E. Mercer. On 13 July 1981, a grey and damp day, the last Winckley pupils, the 1977 intake of 60, walked with their belongings across to Lark Hill, the erstwhile academic rival, for their final GCE year. Back at the school the emptying and stripping had escalated; it had become a hive of destruction. The shock of totally bare classrooms was added to by the noise of shelves being prised off walls and furniture being dragged down corridors and bumped downstairs.

Five
Getting About

Hansom cabs in Fishergate in 1902 by Arthur Winter. During the period between 1885 and 1914 about a dozen firms ran hire transport in the form of landaus and hansom cabs from ranks situated round the town, the largest being outside the Harris Museum. The origin of horse-drawn transport began with Richard Veevers' horse-buses in 1859; other branches and routes were opened up to Ashton, Higher Walton and Walmer Bridge. The horse-tram operation began in 1879 with a route to Fulwood with eight double deck cars running from Guild Week 1882.

Horse-drawn tram, Moor Park near St Thomas's Road, 1903. The leases for the horse-tram system were allowed to run out on 31 December 1903 to introduce an electric system. As a consequence, places like Ashton, Farringdon Park, Fylde Road, Fulwood, Garstang Road and North Road ended up with no public transport when the eight mile operation came to an end. Tin cans were tied to the last horse tram as it trundled home on that evening.

Horse-drawn omnibus, Fishergate in Spring, 1904. There was an immediate outcry for two reasons; fifty men had been thrown out of work and there was no public transport, made worse because the commencement of the electric operation was delayed from March to June 1904. As a result, horse-buses, which still worked out of town routes, were put back on Preston streets for those four months. The routes worked were limited to Fulwood, the Cemetery and Ashton. Oddly enough, no service was run to Broadgate or Farringdon Park.

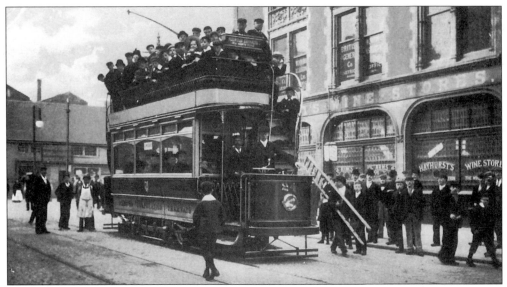

Preston's first electric tram (no.24), 7 June 1904. This is always taken to be the first tram to carry passengers, starting at ten o'clock from the Arcade for Fulwood Barracks, though a car set off at the same time for Farringdon Park. The first routes were the Fulwood Inner and Outer Circles using Watling Street Road, Ashton and Broadgate with additional short workings on the longer routes. The generating plant, with a capability of powering thirty tramcars, was installed in Argyll Road at a cost of £16,000.

Trams in Lancaster Road, 1910. Tram 23 and another, stand at the Fulwood via Deepdale terminus, near two of the controversial tram power cable poles. The first thirty trams were all open top double deckers without canopies, vestibule or direct stairs. All were built at Dick, Kerr and Co. of Strand Road, costing £472 each. The firm went on to produce 8,350 trams, more than any other firm in Britain, between 1898 and 1940.

Tram no.27 in Fishergate, 1931. This tramcar ran from the first day to the last of the tram operation in its original state. The tram operation was a great success. A four week period during the first year showed it had doubled the takings of the horse trams and in December 400,000 passengers were carried, bringing in £2,000. Fifteen cars were enclosed after 1907, the rest by 1912, and in that year three new trams were bought to cope with the low bridge on Fylde Road. About this time applications were made for routes to Walton and up Plungington road.

Tram no.8 in Church Street, 1912. Although this tram looks like it is speeding down Church Street, it is a photographic illusion. From 1906 the maximum speed allowed for trams was 14 mph which was on Deepdale Road. The next highest was 12 mph on the double tracks on Garstang Road: the speed allowed on Church Street was 8 mph. In 1925, the limit was raised to 20 mph; once the fastest vehicle on the road, the tram was now only just keeping up.

Trams 11 and 20, Fishergate 1931. This shows passengers disembarking into the centre of the road. Mr H. Clayton, the general manager, and Mr J. Bamber, the chief inspector, issued a rule book for employees, which forced certain procedures such as keeping trams out of Broadgate when floods were suspected and safety measures near Fylde Road bridge. Employees were to refrain from chewing tobacco, whistling and dancing; they were to be clean and smart, civil to all, help the aged and infirm, and to stop fish and chips from being eaten in their trams.

Football special, tram 18 near the Parish Church, 1930. One of the problems with the tram system was that much of it ran on single track with double track in only a few areas such as New Hall Lane and Garstang Road. In other places loops were set to allow trams to pass, such as in Watling Street Road where there were five. In 1916 an accident occurred at Deepdale on match day when the Northbound track was used as a siding. An inspector left the points open and a tram working the Fulwood Inner Circle crashed into parked tramcars.

Tram 40 in Harris Street, 1930. The Ashton terminus was moved to Harris Street, by the Harris Museum, in 1917, and from here soon afterwards a tram ran away past the General Post Office and down Friargate. The single track was partly responsible for an accident at the Withy Trees in November 1916, when a tram entered a single line in fog and collided head on with the town bound tram in Watling Street Road. The first driver should have waited as he did not have right of way. In May 1934 Tram 6 came off the rails at the County Arms and crashed into a wall, sustaining a great deal of damage.

Leyland Titan bus, Friargate, 1933. By 1930 it had become obvious that buses were more suited to the newly motorised conditions in the town and the tram system would need replanning, but nothing was done. Bus routes operated down Brook Street and Plungington Road in 1922 after many years without public transport. Trams were exchanged for buses on the Ribbleton, Ashton, Broadgate and Farringdon Park routes.

Tram 40 on 15 December 1935. By 1934 the superfluous trams had been sold to other towns, some went to Lytham. More buses were bought and the whole operation ended with Tram 40's last journey. There was no official party, the event was allowed to pass quietly, though, as can be seen, there was a party of sorts. (Spot the stars of stage and screen, J.G.) The system had carried over 370,000,000 passengers in 31 years.

Leyland bus in Garstang Road, 1967. Lack of ambition, lack of foresight and lack of investment at the right time eventually condemned the tram in Preston. The tram routes were used intact until 1969, and the route letters and routes themselves were only changed in 1987. In 1966 Preston Borough Transport changed its colours from a muddy maroon back to blue and white (the horse-trams had been blue) and with the advent of "pay as you enter" the bus conductor disappeared from the buses.

IDENT
SCOTCH EXPRESS
STON. JULY. 13TH 1896. (COPYRIGHT)

Derailment at Preston Railway Station, 1896. By the time of this photograph, the competition between the East and West lines to Scotland was fierce, so fierce that on 15 August 1896, the drivers of a double header express train, pulled by 2159 "Shark" and 275 "Vulcan", who had never been through Preston station non-stop before, drove through far too fast and hit a tight 10 mph curve to the left at 45 mph. The whole train left the rails and both engines leapt and bumped over numerous lines , remaining upright, though the rest of the train was thrown in all directions. the carriages were of a modern construction and remained fairly intact, though battered. There were some injuries but only one passenger was killed . As a result, running times to Scotland on both East and West coast lines were reduced for 36 years, until 1932.

Six

By The Way

St Paul's C of E Church, Park Road, 1903. Now the home of Red Rose Radio, St Paul's, like St Peter's, was a "Waterloo" church and built on land known locally as "The Park". It was opened in 1826, having cost £6,512 and consecrated in the same year. Enlarged in 1882, the church had electricity and an organ installed, donated by Mrs E.H. Booth, wife of the grocery magnate. Like St Ignatius's a short walk away, St Paul's served a heavily populated area and both later had trouble with overflowing graveyards. The church was declared redundant in 1973 and was bought for the radio station after eight years of dilapidation.

Tram 28 by the cemetery gates, 1905. The cemetery, an area of 45 acres, was opened in July 1855, at a time of great need. During the period 1840 -1855, 2,000 people died every year, nearly one in 29 of the town's population. Church graveyards were no longer coping and in some places were disgusting. During the 1840s there was an obnoxious stink around St Paul's as many graves had coffins at surface level and local people were ill. There was a similar problem at the Parish Church. During the period 1842-8, ten thousand Prestonians died, with most burials taking place at the Parish Church (847), St Peter's (2,535), St Paul's (3,579), St Wilfrid's (922), and St Ignatius's (1,550); space was rapidly being filled up.

The Sword of Sacrifice, Preston Cemetery, 1920. This Cross, similar to ones in War Cemeteries all over the world, was erected in 1920 to commemorate the dead of the 1914-18 War and stands on the main path. During the Edwardian period the three sections, Anglican, Free Church and Catholic were run by sextons who lived in lodges by the main gate. At weekends, the cemetery was a mecca for visitors and special trams were laid on from 1904, continued as a bus service until about 1965. In 1882 the Medical Officer of Health, Dr H.O. Pilkington, stated that Preston had one of the highest death rates in Britain. By the end of 1883, over 65,000 had been buried at the cemetery - church grounds would never have coped.

Aerial view, the cemetery and Brockholes Wood Area, 26 April 1948. Designed in the shape of a butterfly, the Old Cemetery has paths laid out as walks and the three chapels, demolished in the mid 1960s, stand out distinctly. On the left, across Miller Road, is the more business-like layout of the New Cemetery. Its 26 acres were bought in 1909 and opened for interments in March 1926. By 1995 there had been 248,181 burials in 42,683 private graves, with an additional nearly 9,000 public graves whose incumbents are uncounted. The photograph also captures a number of post-war developments. In the top left corner are half-built houses on the Grizedale Crescent/Pope Lane estate with roads laid out for further development. To the right, across Brockholes Woods, the complex of avenues, named after English Lakes, on Brockholes Brow. Just below this are houses being built on Farringdon Crescent. Most of the picture is bisected by Miller Road, and in the centre is Ribbleton Hospital, formerly known as Chestnuts Sanatorium, built in 1920 for victims of TB.

THE STRAND, PRESTON.

E 02865

Watery Lane/Strand Road/Water Lane Junction, 1910. In the centre, facing each other, are the Grand Junction at 7 Watery Lane (built 1855) and the Wheatsheaf at 50 Water Lane (built 1857) which lost its name as part of a gimmick in 1994. Its proximity to the dock made it a centre for maritime businesses such as timber merchants, china clay merchants, ship-owners, chandlers, ship-stores and all kinds of dock management. The photograph was probably taken on a Sunday and gives a false impression of peacefulness, but this open junction now pays host to four traffic islands and ten sets of traffic lights.

CAUGHT IN THE ACT.

Haslam Park Gates 1914. This park, an area of 56 acres, was donated by Mary Haslam in memory of her father, John, and was opened in 1910. To the left is the smoke from a train on the Blackpool line which flanks the park and half of which now carries the Preston circular by-pass. The avenue is lined by lime saplings which are now luxuriant and mature. Nowadays, heavy traffic thunders past on Blackpool Road, the arterial road built in 1926 to relieve the town centre of Fylde traffic, connecting Serpentine Road, Addison Road, and Long Lane. Along its three mile length three bridges were built.

St Michael's C of E Church and Tulketh Road c.1912. St Michael's was built in 1908, at a cost of £8,000, in Longridge stone. It started as an adjunct to the much older St Andrew's a mile away and had one of the wealthiest districts in Preston being situated in the rich suburb of Ashton. It finally became a parish in 1926. In the neighbouring avenues lived builders, quarry owners, and industrialists, five of whom were justices of the peace and five were councillors. The horse-trams had served this area using Tulketh Road, Wellington Road, Tulketh Avenue, Beech Grove, and Newton Road. It is worth noting that Fulwood (1859) and Ashton (1879) had public transport many years before poorer areas like Brook Street and Plungington Road (1922).

Waterloo Road, Ashton, 1907. The building of the arterial road in 1926 and the construction of the bridge over the railway destroyed the peace and quiet of this area, with traffic running behind this camera position. In the early 1970s this end of the road was replanned, now the road runs to the left. When the electric tram operation began, Waterloo Road was planned to be part of a circle like the Fulwood arrangement. This, however, was never completed and the terminus was removed to Tulketh Road to prevent trams from having to reverse into Long Lane.

Moor Park Avenue, looking towards Deepdale c.1920. When the area of the Park was limited on the East and West sides, the Avenue, then known as "Ladies' Walk", was defined as its Southern limit, although the Moor carried further on. Serpentine Road (now Blackpool Road) was the Northern boundary. Through the trees can be seen the Grammar School and at the end are the Park gates on Deepdale Road. Beyond , in the 1870s was Deepdale Farm, where a field was rented to a cricket team called Preston Nelson, who had used a pitch on the Park for a season. Changes of sport and name, to football and Preston North End came shortly afterwards - and they are still using that field.

Moor Park Avenue looking towards Garstang Road, 1903. Anthony Hewitson described the Avenue in 1883 as "... attractively bordered with trees, and for driving or riding is very pleasant and agreeable." This is the residential part where the wealthy have lived. The most colourful of these must have been "Will Onda", later Alderman Hugh Rains, of number 15. After an injury finished his career, he promoted films in Preston; among the venues were the Theatre Royal which became a cinema and The Hippodrome which did not.

Moor Park, the West Lodge, Garstang Road, 1905. John Jenkinson, the Park Superintendent, stands at the Lodge back door overlooking the Park. This and the East Lodge were put up in 1833 with the North Lodge on Serpentine Road following three years later. The Park covers 110 acres and before 1833 it was very much a moor where freemen could pasture their animals on land granted to them by Henry III in 1253. Matthew Brown (died 1883) was the last tenant of an agricultural patch in the centre.

Moor Park, North Lodge and Serpentine, 1903. Known plainly as the Duck Pond, the Serpentine was a favourite place to promenade in the thirty or so years before the Park was opened in 1867. It was set out with bowling greens, cricket pitches, new walks and flower gardens. The layout was based on designs by E. Milner of London, who planned Avenham and Miller Parks round the same time. George Rowbotham, the first Park Superintendent, oversaw the work of draining marshy areas, levelling rugged land, creating flower beds and planting shrubs, which all cost nearly £11,000.

Moor Park, the open air baths in 1907. The first Saul Street Baths, opened in 1851, could no longer cope with Summer crowds, so a pool was opened here in June 1907. The pool, measuring 32 yards by 16 yards, 3 to 4 foot 6 inches deep, was surrounded by high banking and bushes to give swimmers privacy. At first, changing took place in a tent although proper facilities were quickly built after uninvited "observers" appeared during ladies' sessions. There was no mixed bathing. The water came from the main supply, and because it was not chlorinated, it was discharged after use into the Duck Pond nearby.

Moor Park, The Swings, 1906. The Children's Recreation Ground was opened in March 1886 and seems to have been an afterthought. It is perhaps an indication of how children were regarded, though evidence suggests there were large numbers of them. The 1911 Census showed that one person in three in Britain was a child under fourteen. The area was set out with swings of different sizes, segregated by sex, see-saws and roundabouts with animal figures. Many children would be left to their own devices as far as play was concerned, if they had time for it. Many lacked toys and so improvised games using everyday items. Moor Park Swings would be a real treat.

The Garrick's Head, 270 North Road, c.1955. In 1868 there were five alcohol licence applications, 278 of which were for beerhouses, where only beer was sold. The Garrick's Head was one of these until about 1950. These places were licensed very cheaply; before the 1904 Licensing Act the fee was only two guineas. In 1868 there was one public house to 167 Prestonians; after the 1872 Licensing Act it fell to one to 273. The 1904 Act reduced the number of licensed premises in North Road from 23 to 14, and among those lost were the The Morning Star, The Iron Duke, The Old Royal George, and The Rose and Crown. The Garrick's Head was demolished during the clearances of 1964.

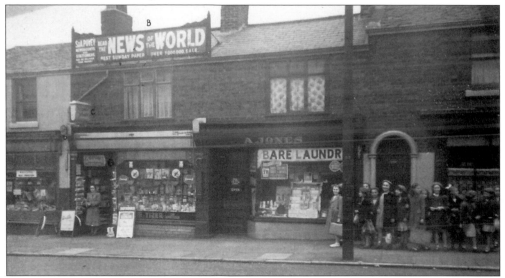

North Road between Sleddon Street and Acton Street c.1955. A class of pupils from English Martyrs' School are in North Road on their way from Saul Street Baths. North Road, almost a mile in length, was home to tightly knit communities clustered round churches and local loyalties to shops, of which there were dozens of different types. As well as butchers, grocers, confectioners and greengrocers, there was a dairy, a clogger, a watchmaker, a tripe shop and a fishing tackle shop. The author's grandparents, Austin and Ann Myerscough ran a newsagents at number 360. This area was demolished in 1964 and is now occupied by commercial units.

North Road Post Office 9 December 1964. Ready for demolition, this once centre of a community is a symbol of the area's shift in character from a centre of population to a place where hardly anyone lives. North Road was an important route from which many side-roads branched, such as Ann Street North, Frank Street, Southgate, Bushell Street, and Broomfield Mill Street. Many houses had been built in the period 1850-1880 and the Corporation was convinced, for heath and financial reasons, that they had to come down.

Moor Lane leading to Sydney Street c.1955. Sydney Street ran from Moor lane, behind the Northern end of North road and emerged into St Thomas's Street by the church. Demolition had begun in 1955 in areas round Manchester Road and Avenham Lane, and in the nine years leading up to 1964, 436 families had been rehoused. Demolition on North Road, Lancaster Road, and Walker Street began on 1 April 1964 and 182 families were to be rehoused in the new estate at Ingol, with another 27 to find their own premises. As far as Sydney Street was concerned, 124 families had to be rehoused. A year later another 1,145 families would need rehousing from Adelphi Street.

The Junction of North Road with Meadow Street and Park Road c.1955. The car on the left is entering Meadow Street while the road stretching away is Park Road: two of the spirelets on St Paul's Church can just be glimpsed through the chimneys. North road and its junction with Walker Street would be to the right. All this was demolished in 1964 to make way for Ringway, the dual carriageway ring road to the North of the town centre. Of all the buildings in Park Road, only the former St Paul's Church survives. In February 1965, *The Lancashire Evening Post* reported many large piles of bricks, described as eyesores, lying around in Walker Street, Lancaster Road and North Road, encouraging petty lawbreaking in premises still standing and hindering police work. In June 1967 Cyril Heywood of the *Post* commented, "As we look disconsolately on the rubble strewn on the demolition sites on which the Preston of the future is taking shape, we should take heart that we are not the only Prestonians who have seen their town laid to waste to make way for what optimists always feel will be better days to come." Many Prestonians feel they never came.

Corner of Garstang Road and Aqueduct Street, August 1953. Aqueduct Street is in the foreground, note the absence of traffic lights. On the left is Garstang Road, running further on into Moor lane. Round the corner from the hoardings is the Albert Billiard Hall. Further along, past the Garstang Road hoardings was Mather's Printers whose premises were finially demolished in September 1995. On the hoardings the top row advertise fairly commonplace items, but the others are more local and advertise events commencing on 7 September 1953. The Empire cinema was about to show an "adults only" feature for that week. The Empire started as a revue theatre in 1911, showing occasional films and was a permanent cinema from 1930 to 1964 when it became a bingo hall and was demolished in 1974. The Palace, advertising a revue, was built on the site of an old skating rink in Tithebarn Street and opened in 1913 as a theatre, though it did show films at times. It was closed in 1955, lay empty and derelict before being demolished to make way for the new Bus Station in 1967. The Royal Hippodrome is advertising another play by the Salberg Players during its successful eight year residence there. The Harris Institute is putting forward its new year of educational courses and the Royal Liverpool Philharmonic Orchestra were about to make one of its regular visits to the Public Hall.

Seven

Guild Days
And Walking Days

Guild Arch, Garstang Road by Moor Park, 1902. During the 1902 Guild, as had been the custom in times past, "welcome arches" were placed at strategic points over main roads to proclaim the Guild to visitors and show Prestonians' pride. This arch was set out as a garden with flower boxes, evergreen arrangements, palms, swags and flags, all making a colourful impression, and surmounted by a motto connected with the celebrations. Through the arch can be seen a grandstand for viewing processions and beyond is the silhouette of English Martyrs' church with mill chimneys in the background.

Guild Arch in Fishergate by the Theatre Royal, 1902. This arch was a solid, British affair with the Royal coat-of-arms at its summit. The area around it is festooned with banners, bunting and floral garlands, showing, again, Prestonian pride in these once in a generation celebrations. During this week 31 August to 6 September the Preston Amateur Operatic Company put on two Gilbert and Sullivan operas. *Iolanthe* was performed daily at 6-30 and *The Yeomen of the Guard* was presented at 9.30, except on the Saturday when the Torchlight Procession took place.

Guild Arch, Church Street near the Parish Church, 1902. This is a Japanese-style arch overseen by the Lamb and Britannia and surmounted by a globe showing the British Empire. Across the top is the legend "Long Live The Guild Mayor and Mayoress" who were the Earl and Countess of Derby (family name Stanley). During the week there were some serious music performed by the Halle Orchestra with Lady Halle playing solo violin in two concerts and Max Bruch in another. Also at the Public Hall, the 300 strong Preston Choral Society choir sang *The Spectre's Bride*, *Hiawatha's Wedding Feast* and *Elijah*, all conducted by Luigi Risegari.

Guild Arch in Adelphi Street by Victoria Street, 1902. The Japanese style of this arch is also reflected in the lamps over the street. The weather during the week was good, so the celebrations and processions went ahead with no problems. All of this area was demolished during 1965-6, having been full of shops, pubs and general stores. Housing in Adelphi, as the area was known, was built around 1850 and was primitive compared with later houses, especially with regard to sewage disposal. Improvements were made between 1899 and 1901 after outbreaks of Smallpox in 1888 and Typhoid in 1897. It is surprising that only two doctors lived close by, one in Plungington and one in Fylde Street.

Guild Arch at Adelphi Street and Fylde Street corner, 1902. The style of this arch was a Chinese footbridge topped by a small pavilion. All the canvas covering was painted in oriental colours with Chinese lanterns and garlands, "May Preston Prosper" is its motto. To the left is the Adelphi Hotel which was established there in 1777. In the Edwardian period there were twenty two pubs within easy reach, There were also eight fish and chip shops, two eating houses and a bakehouse. Places of work were also near; in the same area were nine cotton mills and a biscuit factory.

Guild Arch at Stanley Street, 1922. This much talked about arch of cotton bales is said to have cost Horrockses the cotton manufacturers £15,000. Because of cheap labour this prosperous era was shortlived, worsened by lack of investment in new machinery. In Horrockses' new weaving shed, four hundred sat down to a Guild lunch one day. In the Trades' Procession, some floats carried slogans urging new uses for textile to extend "King Cotton's Domain". In the same procession a Cotton Princess walked with a train of Horrockses cotton sheeting, carried by seven small girls.

Guild Trades' Procession, 3 September 1902. This float' seen in Ribbleton Lane opposite Barton Street, is carrying a soap sculpture carved by the employees of Joshua Margerison and Co. at their White Windsor Soapworks at Leighton Street, near St Walburge's church. This procession is always one of the largest, most varied and colourful of the Guild, with trades and professions showing off their achievements and accomplishments. This procession was split into four sections: Miscellaneous, Building, Engineering and Textile. Some trades represented included hay binders, tobacco spinners and lamplighters. The Official record described the occasion as "...one of very striking character and magnitude".

Guild Trades' Procession, 6 September 1922. Before Guild Week started, the organisers of this procession claimed that it would eclipse anything else seen at previous Guilds or anywhere in the country, ever. Over a hundred vehicles, twenty five bands and several thousand operatives would make up a trades exhibition on the move. Producing industries showed their manufacturing processes from raw material to finished product, the largest being the textile trade which had fifty exhibits and eight bands. The photograph shows exhibits 2, 3, and 4 of the Woodcutting Machinists' display. The contents of the Trades' Procession was described in the Official Record as "brilliant and ambitious", and occupied twelve pages in the official programme.

St Mary's C. of E. Procession New Hall Lane c.1905. St Mary's walkers are returning to church, passing Wilbraham Street (opposite) and Surrey Street corners. Cotton mills in the distance are on Rigby Street and Tennyson Road. St Mary's was opened in 1838 and continues its work today. Its parish was so heavily populated that for a long time more people walked on Whit Mondays than with any other church, and in the 1882 Guild, 2,221 people walked. The whole town took Whit Walks (started in 1844) seriously; it was an enjoyable time. About 1900 Anglicans made up half of the population, Catholics over a third and the rest were Free Church.

Our Lady Statue Whit Monday 1 June 1914. The statue was copied from an original in Chartres Cathedral and carved specially in 1913 for St Wilfrid's men to carry. When he heard of this, the Chief Constable feared trouble, thinking that it might be attacked. Until 1850 Protestants and Catholics in Preston had lived in relative harmony, but Irish immigrants of both persuasions sharpened differences. Fighting during the 1868 Whit Week and severe physical attacks on the 1882 Guild and 1888 Whit Monday processions by Orangemen, and the fact that the police had to stop the Town Hall clock to prevent processions meeting, at least once, caused his concern. The statue was carried with a police presence. The author helped to carry the statue in the 1992 Guild Ecumenical Procession.

Guild Week, Wednesday 5 September 1922. The Catholic Procession is in Fishergate and the live tableau of Stella Maris (Our Lady, Star of the Sea) has reached Avenham Street. The centrepiece is a girl from St Walburge's Women's Guild, carried by a team from the Men's Guild, one of whom is the author's grandfather, Austin Myerscough. He is in the centre, looking to his left. He survived the War, but was injured at Passchendaele in 1917. The Catholic Procession that day had 7,400 participants, carrying 56 banners, and supported by 25 bands.

Eight

Three Days
At The Pageant

Guild Pageant, the third day audience, 1922. This is a section of the crowd on Avenham Park from the North Union Bridge to a stand occupied by Dick Kerr's Band. The excellent Children's Pageants of 1952, 1972 and 1992 all had a magnificent precedent which sealed the importance of children in the Guild (see the Introduction). Only four years after the greatest bloodbath in history, the Great War, the Corporation, backed by popular demand, decided to proceed with the Guild, as it had in troubled times in the past. In 1922 the Guild was a tonic, and one of the most memorable events of the week, still talked about seventy years later, was this Pageant.

Mr A.J. Berry M.A., Master of the Pageant. The Guild Committee wanted a change in children's involvement, one which was a spectacle for large numbers of spectators, so they consulted A.J. Berry, Director of Preston Education and author of *Proud Preston's Story* (1912), and the headteachers of the town. A pageant was chosen to be devised by Mr Berry and produced with the help of teachers and parents. Mr Berry's main aim, in a world "trying to reconstruct its social fabric and rebuild what was shattered", was that Preston's children should follow the Guild principles of working together. In organising the music, art, and acting, the Pageant cut across many social barriers.

Master of the Pageant's Heralds. These boys were pupils from Grimshaw Street School who accompanied Mr Berry during the recital of his Prologues. The Pageant was to be staged in three parts on consecutive days and most of the children involved had suffered some loss during the War, but the zeal with which they participated and the enjoyment which resulted from it obvious from these photographs. The theme was the Guild's history from 660 to 1600, ending with a pageant of Empire. In the Park, the banking by the Belvedere, accommodated the bands, choir and chorus, with 7,000 seats set out for spectators. The weather was poor leading up to the time and rehearsals were constantly interrupted.

Day 1: Thursday 7 September 1922, St Wilfrid and his Attendants. During the early afternoon the clouds melted away and the Pageant began in sunshine. At 2.30pm the Guild Mayor and Mayoress, Mr and Mrs Astley-Bell, were greeted by thousands of applauding spectators and children. The first scene shows Ripon at Easter 661, when St Wilfrid asked for a volunteer to build a church at Preston. The Choir sing an evening prayer to the melody of Gounod's *Ave Maria*.

Day 1: Saxons at Preston. This rough looking group are a band of Saxon hunters, fishermen and falconers. For a time these boys from St Ignatius's School showed the way of life of Preston's early settlers: boatbuilders showed the importance of Fulwood Forest and the Ribble, and potters prepared clay for rough walls in wattle and daub houses.

Day 1: Boniface arrives at Preston. Boniface, St Wilfrid's volunteer, accompanied by monks, meets groups of Saxons working in the fields and village. They agreed to build a church and a time of peace began, symbolised by the Choir singing O *Gladsome Light* by Sir Arthur Sullivan. Up to this point, St Ignatius's schoolchildren performed the action. Pageant photographs were taken during performances and the dress rehearsal. This was at the latter.

Day 1: The Viking Raid on Preston. As the choir sang *The Soldiers' Chorus*, by Gounod, townsfolk took their tithes to the Tithebarn. Meanwhile news came that Vikings had sailed up the River Wyre and burned St Michael's. The people feared for themselves and the town and the shout went up, "Black ships in the Ribble". Through the trees on Riverside there swarms a horde of vicious Viking warriors with murder and pillage as their objectives.

Day 1: Preston priest murdered by Vikings! The priest confronts the wild Viking pack (pupils from Deepdale Road Council School) and is cut down viciously. Each invader carried off items from the town and made their way, gleefully, through the trees to the River. It was later noted by many people how enthusiastically the Deepdale children took their parts.

Day 1: The townspeople discuss future plans. The survivors met in the Market Place to discuss plans for the future and form a Peace Guild for everyone's mutual benefit. At this the Choir sang *Fraternity* by Mendelssohn and *Ode To Joy* by Schubert. In the following episode, rejoicing was followed by dismay after the news of the Battle of Hastings, but the Norman baron, who came to Penwortham looked favourably on the Guild - and on its paying for the privilege. Children from Roebuck Street, Eldon Street, St Wilfrid's and St Walburge's Schools performed this episode.

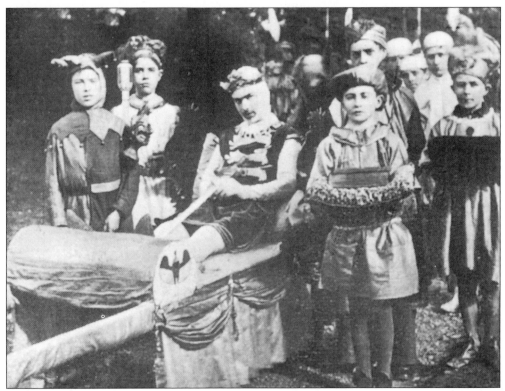

Day 1: King Edward I, played by Ernest Gilleade. The Market Place was cleaned in anticipation of the visit of King Edward I (played by E. Gilleade of St Ignatius's Central School). Out came banners, pedlars, jugglers, jesters and minstrels; fine displays of singing and dancing were made for the King. Although he was ill and carried on a litter, there was much regal splendour. Then local archers in great numbers rallied to the Royal banner to fight the Scots. These, the ladies in the King's retinue, the citizens and their children were all from St Stephen's and St Ignatius's Schools.

Day 1: The Singing of the *Storm*. After the King's departure, news came of his death and the English defeat at Bannockburn. Robert Bruce and his army (from St Andrew's School) burst onto the scene from Top Walks and burned the town after finding little to plunder. Unfortunately no photographs exist of this episode. When the Scots had gone the citizens emerged as the Mayor and Corporation decided to use Guild money to help those who had lost the most. A celebration was held and *The Storm* by John Hullah is sung to signify the town's resurgence. These later scenes were sung and performed by St Saviour's, St Augustine's, St Matthew's, St Mary's C of E, and St James's Schools. The official attendance for this first day was 22,485.

Day 2: Friday 8 September 1922, Medieval Guildsmen. This group, and the next, were pupils of the Catholic College; among them are aldermen and chaplains and the main banner is of the Merchant Taylors. At 2.30pm Mr Berry, accompanied by heralds, read a short prologue to 2,000 performers, 200 choir and chorus, and 18,720 spectators. The day's action spaned the Middle Ages to the reign of Elizabeth I, and included "gorgeous scenes and magnificent costumes" (*Lancashire Daily Post*). The first scene shows the annual Guild festival, beginning with *Awake My Soul* Psalm 133 to a Mozart melody and *Sing Ye To The Lord* set to Jacob Arcadelt's *Ave Maria* melody.

Day 2: Medieval Guildsmen - second group. Another set of College boys, photographed at school, showing the banner of the Cordwainers, the important leatherworkers' guild. In the serene atmosphere created by the hymns, the Guildsmen made their way to church, eventually moving to the arena's centre to gather at the Festive Board. They showed the solidarity and purpose of the Guild by passing round a loving cup of wine and distributing alms to the poor from Guild money.

Day 2: The Angels from the Mystery Play. Suddenly the Bellman or Town Crier appeared and proclaimed the performance of a Mystery Play. There followed a memorable "pageant within a pageant", performed by girls from Winckley Square Convent School, namely the play *Angels and Shepherds* originally enacted in medieval York. The Angels in shimmering white robes (made at school; the wings created at Maitland Street Woodwork Centre) appeared at Top Walks and moved slowly down the slopes to *Hark The Herald Angels Sing*, sung by Choir and Chorus.

Day 2: The Nativity Tableau. This grouping was meticulously based on a tapestry at Exeter College in Oxford designed by Sir Edward Burne-Jones. Its parts were played by Alice Jackson (St Joseph), Lily Hepwell (Our Lady) and the cherubs by Mary Hall and Mary Yates. The platform holding the Nativity Tableau was pulled into the arena as the Shepherds moved in from the Western side to a camp fire.

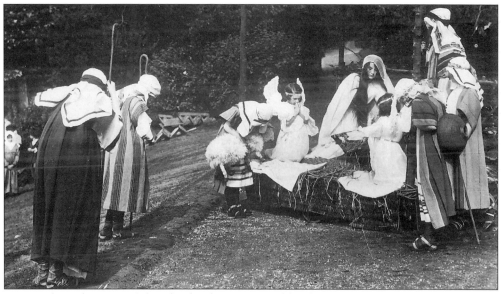

Day 2: The Adoration of the Shepherds. Summoned by the Angels, the Shepherds approach the Crib. Offerings were made as the Choir sang *Sleep Holy Babe*. At this point Avenham Park was suddenly lit by strong sunshine. *The Lancashire Daily Post* commented that this was " the most admired production of the festival ...listened to in rapt attention ...a scene of unalloyed peace...". As the scene slowly changed, the Choir and Chorus sang *When Comes The Reign Of Eternal Peace?* and Wagner's *Pilgrim's Chorus*. Thus ended the episode staged by the Catholic College and Winckley Square Convent School.

Day 2: The Abbot of Whalley. This episode, portraying troubled times was performed by Preston Grammar School with St Saviour's and St Matthew's. The Parish Priest, the Abbot of Whalley and the friars of Greyfriars in Friargate discussed Henry VIII's plans to seize religious property. On being ordered to leave, the friars and monks were begged not to go, by the ordinary people, who then asked for their blessings. Suddenly there was rebellion in the air as the citizens wanted to revolt.

Day 2: Lord Derby's Army. At this point Lord Derby and his men arrived, the boys looking as convincing as the photograph shows. *The Lancashire Daily Post* said they made "…an imposing and glittering martial picture…its stateliness was convincing…". The Mayor asked for the Guild to be preserved. Lord Derby agreed but demanded loyalty to the King or the Guild would be lost. Eventually the property was confiscated, though the Town Council was determined to keep the Guild.

Day 2: The Jesters. The downcast citizens, having lost their Guild property and rights are cheered up by a large group of jesters (from St Walburge's and St Wilfrid's) who, with humorous antics, provided entertainment for the spectators. Mr C.F. Howard, Head of Emmanuel School and conductor of the Chorus wrote the Jesters' Song *There's A Good Time Coming* and the whole episode earned a special mention in *The Yorkshire Post*.

Day 2: Queen Elizabeth meets The Mayor of Preston. Outside Greenwich Chapel, the Mayor and his party wait to greet the Queen. She agreed to renew and extend charters granted by her predecessors. Scenes of great joy greeted the Mayoral party back in Preston. Miss Hague, as the Queen, was dressed in a gold crown, crimson velvet and gold tissue, waited on by richly clothed courtiers. The proceedings of Day 2 came to an end and *England* by Sir Hubert Parry was sung by all. During the day it was decided that the Pageant was so successful that it would be repeated the following week.

Day 3: Saturday 9 September 1922 The Fair. The final part of the Pageant was opened by Mr Berry and his heralds in front of 37,735 spectators, although he later claimed it was over 60,000. The proceedings opened with a fair, a special market, which incorporated a number of activities both useful and frivolous. Booths were put up showing distinct streets for different trades such as butchers, fishmongers, bakers, leather goods and others.

Day 3: The Punch and Judy Show. The creation of the Fair and its equipment was done by the Technical School, and the traders came from Ribbleton Avenue Wesleyan School. Punch and Judy was one of the set pieces of the Fair. The suspended glove in the background marked the Mayor's opening of the proceedings.

Day 3: Merrie England. There was a celebration of Merrie England which began with children from Deepdale Council Infant School plaiting the Maypole. At different times children from the same school acted out nursery rhymes to illustrate aspects of life in the past.

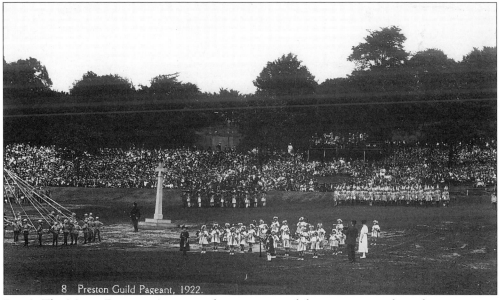

Day 3: The Morris Dancers. A nursery rhymes suggested domestic scenes from the past, games and dances were also revived. Children from Grimshaw Street School, trained by their teachers, gave an exhibition of old morris dances.

Day 3: The rush bearing scene. There was a change in atmosphere from fun to gravity as children advanced to the church doors singing a rush bearing hymn, asking God for strength and prosperity. *O grant us Lord thy blessing, of love and earthly peace.* Recitations and songs about the town and Guild ended the Pageant proper. The schools participating were Hincksman Memorial School and English Martyrs' Central, under the direction of Miss Gardner, the Pageant's Dramatic Adviser.

Day 3: The Union Jack and Rose of Lancaster. The Pageant of Empire began as 3,000 boys in red, white and blue caps move in from all points to the foreground of the arena to form a living Union Jack. At the same time 4,000 girls held up coloured cards which altogether formed a Lancashire Red Rose and the Preston coat-of-arms. Children representing the Home Countries and countries of the World marched into view and grouped round the Union Jack.

Day 3: The USA Tableau. This group are from Moor Park Wesleyan School, characterising famous Presidents, the Pilgrim Fathers and Indians. In the final presentation all races were represented: the colonial countries represented the Empire, with India and the USA next to the Preston group because of the cotton connection. Also represented were the other thirty one Prestons in the world. After hymns and songs praising the town and Guild and a speech of thanks by the Guild Mayor, the Pageant ended with a march past and a rendering of *O God Our Help In Ages Past.*

Day 3: Lancashire Witches - Park School For Girls. The Pageant was an unqualified success, witnessed by at least 90,000 people (proceeds to seaside children's homes), due to the selfless contributions made by teachers , parents and children from all schools. Old rivalries between individual schools, sectarian differences and jealousies were forgotten in a massive exercise of great complexity, only made possible by cooperation on a grand scale.

Day 1: Anglo Saxon Prestonians - Roebuck Street School. At the rehearsals, some critics had called it a "kids' show", but it proved to be much more than that. *The Liverpool Daily Post* said "…the choir (and chorus) is one, and though it holds 5,000 children, it sings with one voice…" *The Universe* commented that "by common consent the three days' Pageant - in which the actors were some 11,000 children in the fine natural amphitheatre of Avenham Park, has been set down as one of the most gorgeous displays that has been witnessed in this country."

Day 1: Guildsmen who met Edward I - St Ignatius's Central School. While the action was played out in full view on the park, the slopes and paths by the Belvedere were excellent for massing large numbers of performers. The trees and bushes provided natural stage wings with the roads and terraces being excellent for displays of marching troops and ceremonial processions. Out of sight on Top Walks and Avenham Walk, performers could be dispersed easily. The trees had begun to take on Autumn colours which were complemented by the choir and chorus dressed in red, white and blue.

126

Day 3 Elizabethan Episode: Technical School Pupils. *The Daily Mail* remarked that "the Pageant represents scores of hours of patient loving work on dresses by mothers at home, besides thousands of pounds spent. But it is worth all of it". An American, Mr Joseph A. Parks, an attorney in Boston, said, "This alone is worth crossing the Atlantic to see. Gorgeous! Wonderful! The whole of the United States has never produced anything like it". The Pageant was a memorable triumph, but it is sobering to remember that a good number of these children would be killed in the next war.

Guild Celebrations 1922. This photograph, taken from the *Preston Herald*'s illustrated souvenir, shows the Weaving shed of James Lee and Bros in Eldon Street, with decorations "voluntarily done by and at the expense of the operatives."

Preston Guild, 1902. Crowds, journalists and cameramen await one of the week's processions from the steps of the Town Hall in Fishergate.

Acknowledgements

The majority of photographs used in this book come from my collection. I would like to thank Lawrence Eccles for his gift of Robert Pateson's 1867 Town Hall and Trevor Lloyd for his gift of the Minton Floor photograph. I also appreciate the loan of some photographs by Norman and Brenda Worthington. I would like to thank Phil Garlington, the photographer, for permission to use some unpublished material and the 1982 photograph of shops in Fishergate.

Although I have copies of the early photographs, the originals are held elsewhere. Therefore I would like to thank the Harris Museum for their kind permission to reproduce the photographs on pages 9, 10, 11, 12, 13, 14, 15 (upper), 16, 17 (top), 33 (top), 36 (top), 48 (top) and 93.

I have, in the course of writing the commentaries, consulted the writings of Leo Warren, J.W. Wilkinson, T. Farrell, David Hunt, Anthony Hewitson, A.J. Berry, Sr Winifred Wickens SHCJ, Margaret Burscough, Alban Hindle, T.R.Flintoff, G.W.Heywood, C. Knight and O.S.Nock. I would also like to acknowledge guidance given by the late Eileen Lord SRN, former Senior Nursing Officer at the Infirmary; Leo and Annie Cafferty, for help on the Children's Pageant and Ray Rolley, the Cemetery Superintendent, for statistics.

I appreciate very much the interest of friends, relations and colleagues and Stephen Sartin's friendly encouragement. I would like to thank Michael Flynn, the Headmaster of All Hallows R.C. High School, where I teach, for permission to use the school network to word process the manuscript and for the loan of a computer to complete it. I also very much appreciate the hours of time that Tony Ryan, Head of Maths, gave up when technical problems occurred at a critical time in the manuscript's word processing.

Lastly, and most importantly, I want to thank Nina, my wife, for her patience, encouragement, advice and for giving me the time and opportunity to research and write - even on holiday!

Stock List

(Titles are listed according to the pre-1974 county boundaries)

BERKSHIRE

Wantage
Irene Hancock
ISBN 0-7524-0146 7

CARDIGANSHIRE

Aberaeron and Mid Ceredigion
William Howells
ISBN 0-7524-0106-8

CHESHIRE

Ashton-under-Lyne and Mossley
Alice Lock
ISBN 0-7524-0164-5

Around Bebington
Pat O'Brien
ISBN 0-7524-0121-1

Crewe
Brian Edge
ISBN 0-7524-0052-5

Frodsham and Helsby
Frodsham and District Local History Group
ISBN 0-7524-0161-0

Macclesfield Silk
Moira Stevenson and Louanne Collins
ISBN 0-7524-0315 X

Marple
Steve Cliffe
ISBN 0-7524-0316-8

Runcorn
Bert Starkey
ISBN 0-7524-0025-8

Warrington
Janice Hayes
ISBN 0-7524-0040-1

West Kirby to Hoylake
Jim O'Neil
ISBN 0-7524-0024-X

Widnes
Anne Hall and the Widnes Historical Society
ISBN 0-7524-0117-3

CORNWALL

Padstow
Malcolm McCarthy
ISBN 0-7524-0033-9

St Ives Bay
Jonathan Holmes
ISBN 0-7524-0186-6

COUNTY DURHAM

Bishop Auckland
John Land
ISBN 0-7524-0312-5

Around Shildon
Vera Chapman
ISBN 0-7524-0115-7

CUMBERLAND

Carlisle
Dennis Perriam
ISBN 0-7524-0166-1

DERBYSHIRE

Around Alfreton
Alfreton and District Heritage Trust
ISBN 0-7524-0041-X

Barlborough, Clowne, Creswell and Whitwell
Les Yaw
ISBN 0-7524-0031-2

Around Bolsover
Bernard Haigh
ISBN 0-7524-0021-5

Around Derby
Alan Champion and Mark Edworthy
ISBN 0-7524-0020-7

Long Eaton
John Barker
ISBN 0-7524-0110-6

Ripley and Codnor
David Buxton
ISBN 0-7524-0042-8

Shirebrook
Geoff Sadler
ISBN 0-7524-0028-2

Shirebrook: A Second Selection
Geoff Sadler
ISBN 0-7524-0317-6

DEVON

Brixham
Ted Gosling and Lyn Marshall
ISBN 0-7524-0037-1

Around Honiton
Les Berry and Gerald Gosling
ISBN 0-7524-0175-0

Around Newton Abbot
Les Berry and Gerald Gosling
ISBN 0-7524-0027-4

Around Ottery St Mary
Gerald Gosling and Peter Harris
ISBN 0-7524-0030-4

Around Sidmouth
Les Berry and Gerald Gosling
ISBN 0-7524-0137-8

DORSET

Around Uplyme and Lyme Regis
Les Berry and Gerald Gosling
ISBN 0-7524-0044-4

ESSEX

Braintree and Bocking
John and Sandra Adlam and Mark Charlton
ISBN 0-7524-0129-7

Ilford
Ian Dowling and Nick Harris
ISBN 0-7524-0050-9

Ilford: A Second Selection
Ian Dowling and Nick Harris
ISBN 0-7524-0320-6

Saffron Walden
Jean Gumbrell
ISBN 0-7524-0176-9

GLAMORGAN

Around Bridgend
Simon Eckley
ISBN 0-7524-0189-0

Caerphilly
Simon Eckley
ISBN 0-7524-0194-7

Around Kenfig Hill and Pyle
Keith Morgan
ISBN 0-7524-0314-1

The County Borough of Merthyr Tydfil
Carolyn Jacob, Stephen Done and Simon Eckley
ISBN 0-7524-0012-6

Mountain Ash, Penrhiwceiber and Abercynon
Bernard Baldwin and Harry Rogers
ISBN 0-7524-0114-9

Pontypridd
Simon Eckley
ISBN 0-7524-0017-7

Rhondda
Simon Eckley and Emrys Jenkins
ISBN 0-7524-0028-2

Rhondda: A Second Selection
Simon Eckley and Emrys Jenkins
ISBN 0-7524-0308-7

Roath, Splott, and Adamsdown
Roath Local History Society
ISBN 0-7524-0199-8

GLOUCESTERSHIRE

Barnwood, Hucclecote and Brockworth
Alan Sutton
ISBN 0-7524-0000-2

Forest to Severn
Humphrey Phelps
ISBN 0-7524-0008-8

Filton and the Flying Machine
Malcolm Hall
ISBN 0-7524-0171-8

Gloster Aircraft Company
Derek James
ISBN 0-7524-0038-X

The City of Gloucester
Jill Voyce
ISBN 0-7524-0306-0

Around Nailsworth and Minchinhampton from the Conway Collection
Howard Beard
ISBN 0-7524-0048-7

Around Newent
Tim Ward
ISBN 0-7524-0003-7

Stroud: Five Stroud Photographers
Howard Beard, Peter Harris and Wilf Merrett
ISBN 0-7524-0305-2

HAMPSHIRE

Gosport
Ian Edelman
ISBN 0-7524-0300-1

Winchester from the Sollars Collection
John Brimfield
ISBN 0-7524-0173-4

HEREFORDSHIRE

Ross-on-Wye
Tom Rigby and Alan Sutton
ISBN 0-7524-0002-9

HERTFORDSHIRE

Buntingford
Philip Plumb
ISBN 0-7524-0170-X

Hampstead Garden Suburb
Mervyn Miller
ISBN 0-7524-0319-2

Hemel Hempstead
Eve Davis
ISBN 0-7524-0167-X

Letchworth
Mervyn Miller
ISBN 0-7524-0318-4

Welwyn Garden City
Angela Eserin
ISBN 0-7524-0133-5

KENT

Hythe
Joy Melville and Angela Lewis-Johnson
ISBN 0-7524-0169-6

North Thanet Coast
Alan Kay
ISBN 0-7524-0112-2

Shorts Aircraft
Mike Hooks
ISBN 0-7524-0193-9

LANCASHIRE

Lancaster and the Lune Valley
Robert Alston
ISBN 0-7524-0015-0

Morecambe Bay
Robert Alston
ISBN 0-7524-0163-7

Manchester
Peter Stewart
ISBN 0-7524-0103-3

LINCOLNSHIRE

Louth
David Cuppleditch
ISBN 0-7524-0172-6

Stamford
David Gerard
ISBN 0-7524-0309-5

LONDON
(Greater London and Middlesex)

Battersea and Clapham
Patrick Loobey
ISBN 0-7524-0010-X

Canning Town
Howard Bloch and Nick Harris
ISBN 0-7524-0057-6

Chiswick
Carolyn and Peter Hammond
ISBN 0-7524-0001-0

Forest Gate
Nick Harris and Dorcas Sanders
ISBN 0-7524-0049-5

Greenwich
Barbara Ludlow
ISBN 0-7524-0045-2

Highgate and Muswell Hill
Joan Schwitzer and Ken Gay
ISBN 0-7524-0119-X

Islington
Gavin Smith
ISBN 0-7524-0140-8

Lewisham
John Coulter and Barry Olley
ISBN 0-7524-0059-2

Leyton and Leytonstone
Keith Romig and Peter Lawrence
ISBN 0-7524-0158-0

Newham Dockland
Howard Bloch
ISBN 0-7524-0107-6

Norwood
Nicholas Reed
ISBN 0-7524-0147-5

Peckham and Nunhead
John D. Beasley
ISBN 0-7524-0122-X

Piccadilly Circus
David Oxford
ISBN 0-7524-0196-3

Stoke Newington
Gavin Smith
ISBN 0-7524-0159-9

Sydenham and Forest Hill
John Coulter and John Seaman
ISBN 0-7524-0036-3

Wandsworth
Patrick Loobey
ISBN 0-7524-0026-6

Wanstead and Woodford
Ian Dowling and Nick Harris
ISBN 0-7524-0113-0

MONMOUTHSHIRE

Vanished Abergavenny
Frank Olding
ISBN 0-7524-0034-7

Abertillery, Aberbeeg and Llanhilleth
Abertillery and District Museum Society and Simon Eckley
ISBN 0-7524-0134-3

Blaina, Nantyglo and Brynmawr
Trevor Rowson
ISBN 0-7524-0136-X

NORFOLK

North Norfolk
Cliff Richard Temple
ISBN 0-7524-0149-1

NOTTINGHAMSHIRE

Nottingham 1897–1947
Douglas Whitworth
ISBN 0-7524-0157-2

OXFORDSHIRE

Banbury
Tom Rigby
ISBN 0-7524-0013-4

PEMBROKESHIRE

Saundersfoot and Tenby
Ken Daniels
ISBN 0-7524-0192-0

RADNORSHIRE

Llandrindod Wells
Chris Wilson
ISBN 0-7524-0191-2

SHROPSHIRE

Leominster
Eric Turton
ISBN 0-7524-0307-9

Ludlow
David Lloyd
ISBN 0-7524-0155-6

Oswestry
Bernard Mitchell
ISBN 0-7524-0032-0

North Telford: Wellington, Oakengates, and Surrounding Areas
John Powell and Michael A. Vanns
ISBN 0-7524-0124-6

South Telford: Ironbridge Gorge, Madeley, and Dawley
John Powell and Michael A. Vanns
ISBN 0-7524-0125-4

SOMERSET

Bath
Paul De'Ath
ISBN 0-7524-0127-0

Around Yeovil
Robin Ansell and Marion Barnes
ISBN 0-7524-0178-5

STAFFORDSHIRE

Cannock Chase
Sherry Belcher and Mary Mills
ISBN 0-7524-0051-7

Around Cheadle
George Short
ISBN 0-7524-0022-3

The Potteries
Ian Lawley
ISBN 0-7524-0046-0

East Staffordshire
Geoffrey Sowerby and Richard Farman
ISBN 0-7524-0197-1

SUFFOLK

Lowestoft to Southwold
Humphrey Phelps
ISBN 0-7524-0108-4

Walberswick to Felixstowe
Humphrey Phelps
ISBN 0-7524-0109-2

SURREY

Around Camberley
Ken Clarke
ISBN 0-7524-0148-3

Around Cranleigh
Michael Miller
ISBN 0-7524-0143-2

Epsom and Ewell
Richard Essen
ISBN 0-7524-0111-4

Farnham by the Wey
Jean Parratt
ISBN 0-7524-0185-8

Industrious Surrey: Historic Images of the County at Work
Chris Shepheard
ISBN 0-7524-0009-6

Reigate and Redhill
Mary G. Goss
ISBN 0-7524-0179-3

Richmond and Kew
Richard Essen
ISBN 0-7524-0145-9

SUSSEX

Billingshurst
Wendy Lines
ISBN 0-7524-0301-X

WARWICKSHIRE

Central Birmingham 1870–1920
Keith Turner
ISBN 0-7524-0053-3

Old Harborne
Roy Clarke
ISBN 0-7524-0054-1

WILTSHIRE

Malmesbury
Dorothy Barnes
ISBN 0-7524-0177-7

Great Western Swindon
Tim Bryan
ISBN 0-7524-0153-X

Midland and South Western Junction Railway
Mike Barnsley and Brian Bridgeman
ISBN 0-7524-0016-9

WORCESTERSHIRE

Around Malvern
Keith Smith
ISBN 0-7524-0029-0

YORKSHIRE
(EAST RIDING)

Hornsea
G.L. Southwell
ISBN 0-7524-0120-3

YORKSHIRE
(NORTH RIDING)

Northallerton
Vera Chapman
ISBN 0-7524-055-X

Scarborough in the 1970s and 1980s
Richard Percy
ISBN 0-7524-0325-7

YORKSHIRE
(WEST RIDING)

Barnsley
Barnsley Archive Service
ISBN 0-7524-0188-2

Bingley
Bingley and District Local History Society
ISBN 0-7524-0311-7

Bradford
Gary Firth
ISBN 0-7524-0313-3

Castleford
Wakefield Metropolitan District Council
ISBN 0-7524-0047-9

Doncaster
Peter Tuffrey
ISBN 0-7524-0162-9

Harrogate
Malcolm Neesam
ISBN 0-7524-0154-8

Holme Valley
Peter and Iris Bullock
ISBN 0-7524-0139-4

Horsforth
Alan Cockroft and Matthew Young
ISBN 0-7524-0130-0

Knaresborough
Arnold Kellett
ISBN 0-7524-0131-9

Around Leeds
Matthew Young and Dorothy Payne
ISBN 0-7524-0168-8

Penistone
Matthew Young and David Hambleton
ISBN 0-7524-0138-6

Selby from the William Rawling Collection
Matthew Young
ISBN 0-7524-0198-X

Central Sheffield
Martin Olive
ISBN 0-7524-0011-8

Around Stocksbridge
Stocksbridge and District History Society
ISBN 0-7524-0165-3

TRANSPORT

Filton and the Flying Machine
Malcolm Hall
ISBN 0-7524-0171-8

Gloster Aircraft Company
Derek James
ISBN 0-7524-0038-X

Great Western Swindon
Tim Bryan
ISBN 0-7524-0153-X

Midland and South Western Junction Railway
Mike Barnsley and Brian Bridgeman
ISBN 0-7524-0016-9

Shorts Aircraft
Mike Hooks
ISBN 0-7524-0193-9

This stock list shows all titles available in the United Kingdom as at 30 September 1995.

ORDER FORM

The books in this stock list are available from your local bookshop. Alternatively they are available by mail order at a totally inclusive price of £10.00 per copy.

For overseas orders please add the following postage supplement for each copy ordered:
> European Union £0.36 (this includes the Republic of Ireland)
> Royal Mail Zone 1 (for example, U.S.A. and Canada) £1.96
> Royal Mail Zone 2 (for example, Australia and New Zealand) £2.47

Please note that all of these supplements are actual Royal Mail charges with no profit element to the Chalford Publishing Company. Furthermore, as the Air Mail Printed Papers rate applies, we are restricted from enclosing any personal correspondence other than to indicate the senders name.

Payment can be made by cheque, Visa or Mastercard. Please indicate your method of payment on this order form.

If you are not entirely happy with your purchase you may return it within 30 days of receipt for a full refund.

Please send your order to:

> The Chalford Publishing Company,
> St Mary's Mill,
> Chalford,
> Stroud,
> Gloucestershire
> GL6 8NX

This order form should perforate away from the book. However, if you are reluctant to damage the book in any way we are quite happy to accept a photocopy order form or a letter containing the necessary information.

PLEASE WRITE CLEARLY USING BLOCK CAPITALS

Name and address of the person ordering the books listed below:

_____

_____

_____ Post code _____

Please also supply your telephone number in case we have difficulty fully understanding your requirements.   Tel.: _____ - _____

Name and address of where the books are to be despatched to (if different from above):

_____

_____

_____ Post code _____

Please indicate here if you would like to receive future information on books published by the Chalford Publishing Company.
___ Yes, please put me on your mailing list   ___ No, please just send the books ordered below

Title	ISBN	Quantity
....	0-7524-_____-___	_____
....	0-7524-_____-___	_____
....	0-7524-_____-___	_____
....	0-7524-_____-___	_____
....	0-7524-_____-___	_____
	Total number of books	_____

Cost of books delivered in UK = Number of books ordered @ £10 each =£ _____

Overseas postage supplement (if relevant)   =£ _____

TOTAL PAYMENT   =£ _____

Method of Payment   ❑ Cheque   ❑ Visa   ❑ Mastercard   **VISA**

Please make cheques payable to *The Chalford Publishing Company*   MasterCard

Name of Card Holder   _____

Card Number ❏❏❏❏❏❏❏❏❏❏❏❏❏❏❏❏❏❏❏❏

Expiry date ❏❏ / ❏❏

I authorise payment of £_____ from the above card

Signed _____